Somebody's Knockin'

The Amazing Life
of Terri Gibbs

Official Biography by R. Douglas Veer & Terri Gibbs

First Printing: 2019
ISBN-13: 978-1-7323243-9-8
Library of Congress Control Number: 2019905645

Front Cover Photos: Stock Image by Pexels.com
Photo Courtesy Andrea Ch
Back Cover Photo: Courtesy Candace Morgan

* * * * * * *

Booking Information, Please Contact:
Terri@TerriGibbs.us
Book Ordering: see Amazon.com

Changed Lives Publishing, LLC
Contact Doug@DougVeer.com

DEDICATION

To David, my precious son: Ever since I heard your
heartbeat at nine weeks you have been the joy
of my life. Every good and perfect gift comes from
above and you have been one of those perfect gifts.
I am so proud of the man you have become. No matter
where life takes you, always know that I am your
biggest fan. As Robert Munsch and Sheila McGraw
said in their book, (*I Will Love You Forever*),
"I will love you forever, I will like you for always,
and as long as I'm living, my baby you'll be."
May God richly bless you each and every day.
Love Momma.

To my Lord and Savior Jesus Christ: My heart delights
in You every day. Psalm 37:4 says, ***"Delight thyself
also in the Lord: and he shall give thee the
desires of thine heart,"*** (KJV). Lord, you have
done that for me. I know that the song,
Somebody's Knockin', was a stepping stone in my life
to bring me to this moment that I might be able
to write this book and tell people of Your saving grace.
How ironic that a song that was written about the devil
would ultimately be used to draw people to Jesus.
***"And we know that all things work together for
good to them that love God, to them who are the
called according to his purpose,"*** (Romans 8:28;
KJV). My deepest desire is that people all over the
world will come to know You in a mighty way
through the words written here. And for the ones who
already know You, that they would be encouraged
through these words each day. Lord, You are the light
in my life every day in the darkness. I so look forward
to spending eternity with You.

PREFACE

BELIEVING IS SEEING

The pages in this book will take you on a journey
through the life of Terri Gibbs, and she will tell you
about her experiences in her own words.
You'll read about her birth, her family, and her youth.
She will introduce you to her husband, son, and
daughter. She also has several friends
she wants you to meet like her guide dog, Birdie.
You'll learn how Terri was discovered and promoted
as a Country music icon and shining star
with the encouragement of many music legends
she met along the way: folks like Bill Anderson, Chet
Atkins, Barbara Mandrell, Dick Clark, Ronnie Milsap,
George Jones, Glen Campbell, Merle Haggard, Dolly
Parton, Linda Ronstadt, Anne Murray, Karen Carpenter,
James Taylor, Emmylou Harris, and
Tammy Wynette just to name a few.
Some of the stories here may surprise you;
some will make you laugh; some will make you cry.
But you will enjoy reading this biography
as presented in these pages.

*On another note, the words written here
are not about the truth of being blind,
but about being blind to truth.*

This book will also shed light on the *truths* God wants
to share with you through His Word. God wants the
truth to *set you free*, and He is seeking you out
because He desires to have a close and
intimate relationship with you.

The Apostle John said,
*"And you shall know the truth, and
the truth shall make you free,"* (John 8:32; NKJV).
Another Scripture in Revelation says,
"Behold, I stand at the door, and knock . . ."
(Revelation 3:20; NKJV).

**Terri responded to that knock.
She learned that when Somebody's knockin',
it's best to answer the door.**

INTRODUCTION

THE TERRI I KNOW

Have you ever known someone who made you feel at ease from the first time you met? You know what I mean: good old down-home, country-comfortable; like a lifelong friend. When you meet Terri, you'll feel like you've been friends forever.

There are plenty of folks around today who wouldn't give you the time of day or help keep you from missing a ride to your own wedding. Terri would not only help you catch your ride, she'd offer to drive you herself.

Actually, I have her on video driving a car! Of course, a policeman had stopped her because her driving behavior was rather odd. He stopped her and asked, "Is everything O.K. today?"

She responded, "Yes. Did I do something wrong?"

The officer answered, "Ma'am, you've been driving in a circle for the last thirty minutes."

She reasoned, "Don't blame me. My GPS keeps telling me to make a left turn." She added, "I'm looking for Chubby Checker but I can't seem to see him anywhere!"

I don't think she got a ticket that day. When she told the officer she was supposed to pick up Chubby Checker and give him a ride to the Artists Music Guild Awards Show, he completely understood.

But she's blind, you say? Well yeah! But you don't know Terri like I do. Believe it or not, she has a driver's license! Well maybe it's not a driver's license. It's actually an I.D. card that looks just like a license. I guess that makes it all legal, right?

Anyway, this little video scene was really a "put-on" for one of her stage appearances prior to an awards presentation where she was honored. Yes, Chubby Checker and many others were there that day and it was great fun for everyone to see the clip of Terri behind the wheel.

Terri loves to have fun but at the same time, she's a very serious person. And she's very giving. She would give you the shirt off her back and then ask you what else you needed. I know, I know. That's not *Hollywood!* But then, neither is Terri. So how would you best describe her? Let me say it this way . . .

Some notable songs stand out in my mind when I think of Terri. Barbara Mandrell wrote a song that says, "I was Country when Country wasn't cool". Combine that with, "She's a Lady", by Tom Jones. Now let's add two more song titles to the mix: one is the Stevie Wonder song, "Isn't she lovely". Last but not least, how about that old Gospel song Terri loves so much, "My Jesus I Love Thee."

Now you have the complete picture. Terri Gibbs is a lovely Country lady who loves Jesus, she has a voice of pure gold that's as smooth as butter and she's as sweet as honey from the honey-comb.

I want to make this a very personal story by letting Terri start at the beginning and tell you all about her life. It will start even before she was born, with her mother, her father, and her birth.

I assure you it has not been a normal, run-of-the-mill life. Hiding behind her beautiful smile you'll find loneliness and sorrow you never thought you'd encounter. Terri will also share some of her triumphs, deep thoughts and experiences including how she found the most amazing joy--in a bookstore, of all places.

So listen carefully as she tells you in her own words, about her public and private life. I now present to you, Miss Terri Gibbs.

--*R. Douglas Veer*

CHAPTER ONE
MY HERITAGE

SOUTHERN ROOTS

Although I was born in Miami, Florida, my "Florida life" was short. I was there for only a matter of a few months; I was actually raised at Momma and Daddy's home in a suburb called Grovetown, just outside of Augusta.

In the late 1700s Augusta was the capital of Georgia and in the mid-1800s it was the birthplace of the Southern Baptist Convention. I grew up in the late 50s and early 60s. At that time Grovetown was originally known as the town of Belair. The population was just a little over a thousand people. Yeah, that's "country" alright, but I'm glad to have grown up in the South. I am a "Georgia girl" at heart with "Georgia country" in my blood.

MY MOTHER'S BIRTHPLACE

In the early 1900s Judge William Gibson, a former Colonel and Commanding Officer of the 48th Brigade of the Confederate Army, donated five hundred dollars--which was a lot of money back then--so they could build the first public building in the County of Glascock.

The building was finished August 20, 1913, and still stands on Main Street today as the Glascock County Court House. It's on the National Public Registry of places to visit in Georgia.

Why is this important? Because that's where my momma, Betty, was born, May 16, 1933, in Gibson,

Georgia. Gibson is about 45 miles from Augusta. It was a small town with less than 500 people but it has grown since that time.

MY FATHER'S BIRTHPLACE

While all that was going on down in Gibson, my daddy, Donald King Gibbs, was born October 10, 1934 in Augusta. His family had a farm in the area of Belair Road and Gibbs Road, which was named after his family. All of that land was used to graze dairy cattle. There were no homes; just two hundred and some acres of Granddaddy Gibbs' dairy land, and the highway.

In 1953 Daddy went to work for Western Electric installing telephone lines and communication systems all around the country. Back then, Western Electric was the largest manufacturer of electrical communications equipment in the United States and it was the primary supplier of electrical equipment to both AT&T and the Western Union Company.

MOMMA AND DADDY MEET

Momma's family eventually left Gibson and moved to Augusta. While in high school Momma got her first job at the five-and-ten-cent-store on Broad Street. Later, when she was old enough, she went to work for the telephone company as an information operator. It was through that work connection that Momma and Daddy met and fell in love, and before long Daddy asked her to marry him. She said "yes".

Momma said that after they were married, she quit working for the phone company so she could travel with Daddy when he worked out of town. He traveled for his job which sometimes carried him far away from home. Momma would go with him and they would be gone many days at a time, sometimes even stretching into weeks. Marriage was wonderful for them. Their lifestyle was contented and blissful.

VACATIONLAND USA

In the Spring of 1954, Western Electric sent Daddy to work in Miami, Florida. Although Momma was--by that time--pregnant with me, she went with him anyway because I wasn't due to be born until September which was several months away. So they made the move and settled down to live happily in the Florida sunshine and enjoy the warm sunny beaches.

This was going to be a big change for them compared to life in Belair, Georgia. But it was a good change. They would have all summer to take in what you might call a paid vacation before having to go back home in the fall to get ready for Momma's due date.

Daddy spent a fair amount of time at work but there was plenty of time left over for fun too. Daddy loved the amazing Florida weather. And Momma had several weeks to relax and appreciate life before taking on the role of motherhood.

My parents had also picked out my name. I was going to be called Teresa, which means, autumn harvest. What a great name for a September baby. The harvest of wheat, corn, tobacco, cotton, and pumpkins makes for a beautiful time of year in Georgia and Momma was looking forward to holding her first-born child during this upcoming, season of abundance. Could life be any better than this? Probably not, and this was just the beginning!

CHAPTER TWO
FROM A MOMMA'S POINT OF VIEW – PART I

SETTLING IN

Hi, I'm Terri's momma, Betty. Here's how I remember things. As soon as we got to Miami, we got an apartment right on the main street. Because we had already traveled so much to several states like North and South Carolina and the Virginia's, I hadn't yet seen a doctor to check on my pregnancy. So I found a doctor just at the end of the block.

I remember we had been in Miami for three weeks but I hadn't been able to get much rest. I guess I was stressed from the long trip and the move and so the short of it is that I developed a kidney infection which caused me to develop a high fever. That in turn caused me to go into labor with Terri, three months early.

LIFE AND DEATH

It was June 15th. My labor pains had begun so my husband, Donald, rushed me to the emergency room of St. Francis Hospital in Miami Beach. The medical people were told that I wasn't due until September but it all happened anyway. Terri was born that day weighing only two pounds, eleven ounces.

The doctors said she was so small and underdeveloped that there was no way she was going make it. They weren't giving us much hope. They told my husband that I was in great jeopardy and could possibly die. They didn't expect Terri to live either. That must have been devastating for a young nineteen-year-old husband. The whole situation was very difficult, not to mention that we were alone in a strange city with no family to support us.

Upon waking up--and there in front of everyone--I started to cry. I was still in pain from my illness, and, the doctor was telling us we were going to lose our baby. Donald was crying enough for both of us and if we ever needed a miracle it was right then.

Terri was put into an incubator right away and placed on oxygen. The doctors said they couldn't release Terri until she weighed at least five pounds. On top of that, she was so premature they had to keep her in the intensive care unit. During that whole time, we weren't even allowed to touch her.

Our circumstances led my husband's company to let us stay in Miami until Terri could be moved. All the while the doctors still doubted she would live long enough to be released. Things did not look promising.

GOD INTERVENED FOR US

Hour by hour went by. Day after day passed in expectant agony. The little premature baby whose life seemed destined to slip away still hung on. In the face of all the predictions, death just could not seem to capture her. Imagining the sorrow that loomed ahead, losing Terri weighed heavily on our minds.

In spite of everything, Terri continued to breathe. She was fighting against the impossible as the doctors had basically given up hope. But there she was still kicking and crying. I guess God had His own plan for her which was greater than any medical prognosis.

The hours stretched into days and the days grew into weeks. The weeks grew to more than a month, and still, she continued to fight for her life. Perhaps

God decided to create a miracle to show people what He could do. I know this to be true because the good news finally came.

After two months Terri reached a weight of five pounds. She was better at last and was discharged from the hospital. Donald and I were able to take our baby girl home so that we could be together as a family. Now life was going to be good to us, or so we believed.

Thinking back on it, it was such an ordeal but God worked it out completely. He even sent us some special fiends to lean on. We were so thankful to have the support of an elderly couple who rented their duplex apartment to us when we first arrived in Miami. They had moved from Ohio to Florida to retire and were just the sweetest people in the world. We considered ourselves very fortunate to have such wonderful fellowship with them, especially in our time of need.

MIRACLES ARE REAL

Donald and I were eventually able move back to Georgia once again and settle down. Our lives were full of nothing but pride and joy. I know many people don't believe in miracles, but here she was two months old, very much alive and on her way home. The Lord had healed Terri of what the doctors had abandoned as hopeless. Our tears had turned to smiles and laughter.

I believe that by all medical means she shouldn't have made it. Could the doctors have had any other explanation for her survival? No, I don't think so. Not after announcing to everyone, "She's too small; she's too weak; she's far too undeveloped. She's not going to live . . . she'll probably die." We definitely give God the glory.

MOMMA NOTICED SOMETHING WRONG

All was well and fine for the first few months. Then I began to notice that something was wrong with Terri's eyes. The pupils looked strange as if they were becoming lighter or something. I would wave my hand or some other object in front of her and she didn't seem to respond. We took her to the eye doctor and after examining her he gave me the bad news. My daughter was blind.

Terri was diagnosed with a condition called Retrolental Fibroplasia, which is an abnormal development of the blood vessels in the eyes. It's a condition that quite commonly occurs when premature babies are put into oxygen incubators and are kept in that raw oxygenated environment for too long a period without having their eyes protected.

Unfortunately, the doctors didn't know that back then. Medical science had not yet discovered how such a problem could arise. But in fact, it was a year to the day that Terri was born, that researchers found that over exposure to oxygen inside an incubator could lead to blindness.

While such damage to the blood vessels in unprotected eyes was often the case, blindness didn't always occur. In Terri's situation, she had been exposed to oxygen for two months and that was more than enough time for visual impairment to develop. The doctor's statement was sad but true. The fact remained: my baby had lost her sight.

We wonder why God allows these things to happen. In the book of John, there's a story about Jesus healing a blind man. ***"Rabbi," his disciples asked him, "why was this man born blind? Was it because of his own sins or his parents' sins?"***

"It was not because of his sins or his parents' sins," Jesus answered. "This happened

so the power of God could be seen in him," (John 9:2-3; NLT). Even though Terri has not yet been healed of her blindness, she can still declare the power of God in her life.

Getting back to my story, I asked the Doctor, "What kind of a life will my baby have now that she's blind?"

His answer was, "Well, you can always have other children."

Good grief. Was that it?! "You can have another baby?" Was Terri that unimportant! He might as well have said that she was a *throw-away;* that she could easily be replaced! Was *that* the answer?

In later years I shared this story with Terri. By that time, she had a child of her own and could only imagine how hard it was for me to hear those words, especially coming from a doctor. She couldn't believe he would have said that to me, but he did. Maybe he was trying to comfort me, but at the time, I thought it was a cruel, insensitive thing to say.

I guess he didn't know what to say, but *that certainly wasn't it!* Even so, I knew God had a plan and Terri was nothing less than a blessing. It was heartbreaking for me and Donald but we had to do what was needed to take care of our child. We raised her with all the love and caring we could give her.

CHAPTER THREE
FROM A MOMMA'S POINT OF VIEW – PART II

MAKING MUSIC
We had quite the experience raising Terri. But it wasn't really that hard even though she was blind. She was a good child and she was very satisfied with life. To some degree she was a loner; she had her own things that pleased her.

As a baby, Terri had several different rattlers and I soon found that she would play "music" with them. Of course, at that age she didn't know what music was but in her own way she would play little "melodies" with her rattlers; it was music that only she understood. That's how she entertained herself.

Overall, Terri was a quiet child. I do remember one incident, though, that she had with her cousin when they were about three years old. Terri was delighted over some old spoons that her Grandmother had given her. She would put one or two in one hand and two or three in the other hand and sit there and beat out a "tune" on the cement floor. I guess it was the love of music coming out of her, even back then.

This particular day at her grandmother's house, her cousin reached over and grabbed the spoons away from her. It upset Terri so much that in spite of being blind, she jumped up and grabbed her by her shirt collar. It scared that poor girl to death and she backed away from Terri really fast. She wasn't used to anyone pushing her around or fighting back, especially Terri. I guess it surprised her grandmother and I and made us laugh like crazy because Terri had never expressed that kind of emotion before.

GRANDMOTHER'S SPAT WITH GRANDDADDY

Before we had built our own home, Donald and I lived with his folks on the dairy farm until Terri was four years old. I can remember in those days that Terri used to like to sit on the floor and play. One day, she was playing as usual when she heard her grandparents get into a bit of a spat.

Grandmother was going on and on and on, kind of like, "Blah blah blah". Now Granddaddy was a true *man* if there ever was a man. But this one day, I guess he got fed up; he finally had had enough of her nattering. I heard him very quietly say, "Effy . . . shut . . . up."

She kept talking so Granddaddy once again said, "Effy . . . shut . . . up."

Terri didn't know what was going to happen but the situation didn't seem to be good, so she thought she would try to intervene. She got up and went over to her Grandmother and said, "Grandmother . . . Granddaddy said, 'Shut . . . up!'" It was so funny! Everyone burst out laughing; it tickled everybody in the room. And that ended the argument.

DON AND DALE

At the age of eight, Terri's brother, Don, came along. When Terri was twelve, Dale was born. They loved her very much. When they were babies, she would hold and play with them. She used to sit in her rocking chair and feed Dale his bottle and sing. Terri was a good babysitter. Her brothers enjoyed growing up with her. Even today she teases Dale and says, "Remember, you're still my baby brother".

The kids played together all the time. Terri couldn't tussle with them too much, though, because

20

she didn't know where she was hitting. She actually bloodied Don's nose one day. I guess he never saw it coming.

As Terri's brothers grew older, they realized more and more that she couldn't see, so they would try to hide things from her. But she had a powerful weapon: she could hear! They couldn't understand that but her sense of hearing was truly amazing. She could hear things that we take for granted. Like I tell some folks, she can hear a gnat hiccup. How ridiculous is that?!

When Terri was much older, she asked her daddy one day, "Daddy, if someone broke in on me and I went back in a room and got hold of a gun, would you be afraid of me?"

Without too much thought Donald said, "Well . . . hell yeah!" Terri's daddy was a little rough around the edges, but he was a good man. His answer strongly showed that because Terri could hear so well, she would absolutely be able to point a gun in the right direction and be lethal with it. He had no doubts.

CHAPTER FOUR
FROM A MOMMA'S POINT OF VIEW – PART III

SCHOOL LIFE

I heard about a teacher in Augusta who taught Braille. Her name was Helen Ferrhar. Since Terri was getting close to school age, I thought it would be good for her to teach Terri and it would be good for me to learn it as well so I could help her with her school work.

So, when Terri was five years old, Helen--whom we called Aunt Helen--worked privately with her. Terri always caught on to new things very quickly so she had no problem excelling at Braille. Eventually, she learned to type on a Braille writer as well as a regular typewriter.

The early training through Aunt Helen had advanced Terri to where she only had to attend first grade for the last half of the school year. God was right on time with all of that because the following year, Richmond County School started a new program for the blind and legally blind children in the Augusta area.

The curriculum integrated blind children with sighted children and a special instructor provided a class each day to go over regular course work. The program was a real blessing because it kept Terri from having to move to Macon, Georgia for special needs education. That would have been a three-hour trip as it was 150 miles away. I told Donald that if Terri had to move to the Macon School for the Blind, he better buy me a house next door to it because I couldn't stand the thought of her going away and me not being near her.

Also, the Richmond County School had a counselor who helped Terri with ordering Braille books and helping with course material that Terri might have been troubled with. The counselor supervised all tests and exams as well. Terri benefitted from the program through seventh grade which was all that was required. Later Terri completed her schooling at George P. Butler High School.

Yes, our God is an on-time God. He knew just what Terri was going to need before we did. God *is* good all the time.

DON'T PICK ON *MY* CHILD!

While in elementary school there was one Assistant Resource teacher we didn't like very much. She was hard on Terri and it really upset me when I got wind of it. I learned that she would hit Terri's fingers with a pencil if she misspoke or didn't do what she thought she should. I wasn't about to put up with that! That teacher was being paid to help Terri. And besides, her hands were her eyes!

I reported the woman to the Principle of the school and I guess he must have chewed her out because I didn't have to report anything else about her again. Afterward, she wanted to *apologize* to me but that didn't go over at all. I never had any use for her after that.

I stuck up for Terri when it was called for but she was pretty good at sticking up for herself too. Let me tell you another story on that subject.

NOT KEEPING SECRETS

There was another incident when Terri was in the sixth grade. You know how girls always share their secrets. Well, there was this boy that Terri liked, so she confided in one of the girls at school about it.

The next thing you know the girl told everyone Terri's secret. Terri got quite upset and disappointed. She tried not to be ugly to the girl, but she approached her and asked, "Why did you do that? I didn't want everyone to know."

The girl sneered back at her and said, "If you don't like it, you can meet me outside at recess."

Terri replied, "You got it. I'll be *there!*"

When recess came Terri went outside and the fight was on. But Terri said the girl didn't play fair. First, she lured her out into an area of the schoolyard where they wouldn't be seen. Then she threw a few hard punches, hitting Terri on the arm. Then she slung Terri down on the ground causing Terri to skin her knee. When she came home, I saw right away that she was hurt so I asked her about it. Then she told me the whole story.

Terri received a couple of hits but did manage to get in one good slap; she slapped the girl's face! I wish I would have been there to see it. In spite of Terri's quiet nature, she was not one to be pushed too far, or else it was, "look out." She says there are times when you have to stand up for yourself.

I guess some people are just mean. You can't get anything nice out of them. This girl was a bully and seemed to have a personality problem. Maybe she felt jealous because Terri received so much attention. Maybe she didn't like it and wanted to change things. Well, it sure backfired on her. First, she found out that Terri could take care of herself. Second, when the Principle caught wind of it he dealt with her too.

****

Terri adds, "People with disabilities are not seen for who they really are. Although folks might try to picture themselves in the same situation, they can't imagine how *they* could ever deal with it, so they think *you* can't deal with it either. Everyone has a limit. People can only handle so much. So, if someone is disabled, we have to realize there's still a real person inside of them. And that person, just like anyone else, deserves respect.

"Another thing: folks think that blind people *can't hear* because they *can't see*. And they wonder how in the world blind people can get along. It's harder for people that have had their sight at one time and then lost it, than for those who have no memory of being sighted. But even for those who have lost their sight, they need to remember that they *can* learn to manage and get along. *They can do it.* And *we* need to see them for who they are as a person and not define them by their disability."

CHAPTER FIVE
FROM A MOMMA'S POINT OF VIEW – PART IV

TERRI STRETCHES HER WINGS
The day came when Terri wanted to live on her own. So, we bought a mobile home and Terri moved into it. She was about twenty-two years old at the time.

It was on our property so she would still come over to eat. She had things to eat during the day of course, but she would come over here for supper. The arrangement gave her freedom to practice her piano and read her Braille and do all of the things she enjoyed doing without disturbing anyone over here.

Speaking of cooking, Terri learned a few things from me, but she learned a lot more when she got out on her own. She did easy things though; nothing really complicated. If there was something she wanted to cook she would ask me or someone else how they did it.

When she was at home, I watched her in the kitchen. She was always careful so I never worried about hot stoves or boiling pots. She handled things very well. And I don't remember any bad mishaps, well . . . except for one.

Terri was alone in her mobile home one day. She was opening a can and used to say there was a trick to it that helped her. She said, "If you punch a hole in the top before you open it up enough to pour out the contents, the stuff comes out of the can much more easily. That's because that extra hole lets the air out which is what holds the stuff inside." Terri was quite good at doing this with an ice pick.

Well on this particular day, she went to punch a hole in the can and the ice pick slipped and drove itself into one side of the tip of her finger and protruded out the other side. Terri called me and casually said, "Hey, what cha doin'?"

I told her something or other and she said, "Well, I've had a little mishap over here; could you come over and help me a bit." So, I went over there and saw the ice pick in her finger! We got it out and everything was fine after that. I think that's when I started having heart trouble. (*Just kidding . . . ha ha ha.*) Actually, Terri has done a great job of being on her own.

It's good to look back. Life did have some hard spots but we worked through those times. We had many good times and laughs too. Things weren't always funny but overall, it's been a wonderful experience raising Terri and having her for my daughter. I think Terri has done really well for herself. Even though I always have been and
always will be here for Terri as long as I live, I must say she has accomplished a great deal for herself and has made me a very proud and happy mother.

GOOD HOUSEKEEPING

Terri always had pets around the house. She had several cats and dogs over the years. I remember this one cat she named "Buba". He was bad about crawling under cabinets or being shut in closets. Terri tells the story this way:

"I remember how I would hear Buba meow and would have to figure out where it was coming from. I was doing laundry one day when unbeknownst to me, he decided to climb into the dryer. I put the clothes in and shut the door. I pressed the "on" button and all of a sudden, I heard a terrible yowling sound.

"I immediately realized what had happened and quickly snatched the door open. Buba shot out of the dryer like a cannon. He received a Ph.D. in education that day. He never climbed into anything else from then on. He came to be known as 'Doctor Buba.'"

I remember another time Terri got in trouble when she was house cleaning. Here's how she explains it:

"One day I decided I would give my area rugs a good beating to get the dust out. There was a side door in my mobile home with no steps. I thought it would be the perfect place to do that. I grabbed a rug, opened the door and began shaking it with great gusto.

"Suddenly, I felt a sharp pain on the side of my face. I didn't realize it, but wasps had built a nest over the door. I guess they were as surprised as I was. I received two stings on my face. I had to laugh, though: so much for being 'Suzie Homemaker'. I never did anything like that again without asking questions first."

I AM BLESSED

Terri adds, "I'm blessed to be able to say that Momma was right here all the way. Momma and Daddy did not give up on me.

"First, my parents didn't treat me as a blind child. They brought me up as if I had been sighted. I was sent to regular schools just like other kids.

"Also, I wasn't spoiled. I had chores to do and everything. I had to pull my weight. But it was all good. I guess Momma taught me that I wasn't going to be beaten down by my blindness. I wasn't going to be helpless in a world ruled by the sighted. Instead, I was going to learn how to cope with it so I could live a normal life and know how to do things for myself.

"I'm so glad Momma did that for me. I think I would have missed out on so much if she hadn't raised me the way she did. I thank God for the parents I had.

I could be wrong, but if I had been the blind child of some other parents, I don't know that I would have had the same advantages. I am so grateful.

"I wish my daddy was still with us. He worked for Western Electric from 1953 until 1984. That last year, doctors discovered a problem with his heart and he was only given a few months to live. I was worried that he didn't yet know the Lord. He had been angry with God since my birth because he felt that my blindness could have been avoided. Also, he didn't understand that the Lord had bigger plans for my life. The Bible says, *'And we know that all things work together for good to those who love God, to those who are the called according to His purpose,'* (Romans 8:28; (NKJV).

"I expressed my concern to a friend and we prayed a prayer of agreement together based on Matthew 18:19-20: *'Again I say unto you, That if two of you shall agree on earth as touching any thing that they shall ask, it shall be done for them of my Father which is in heaven. For where two or three are gathered together in my name, there am I in the midst of them,'* (KJV).

Later, she and her husband led my dad to the Lord which was three months before he died. God is so faithful; He honored that prayer and I know I will see him again one day.

"Sadly, my dad was only fifty years old when he died. I spent thirty years of my life with him but I wish we would have had more time together."

CHAPTER SIX
TERRI DANCES TO THE MUSIC

MUSIC TO MY EARS

Now it's time for Terri to share *her* story.

Music came into my life at a very early age. I was still just a baby when I fell in love with those beautiful sounds coming from the piano. All of the musical notes dancing out into the air were like shapes and colors and light that floated their way into my world of darkness.

Whenever I heard my grandmother sit at the piano and play, I was thrilled beyond anything I could put into mere words. The sounds reached deep into that special place inside of me that touched the chords of my life. It filled in the missing parts of me that could not see.

Music is a universal language. Just think, how often do you hear something so beautiful that you lean back and close your eyes to take it in? It's magical when you shut everything out except the beautiful soundscapes that enter your heart. That's the kind of glory I would capture as I heard those amazing melodies flow from the piano into my very being.

You know I've never been into drugs or alcohol or anything like that. I've never tried them nor did I ever want to. But the truth is that I love music so much that when I hear the beauty of it, it's like I'm connected to another world. Yes, music is wonderful. It takes me to another universe. And nothing in the world of drugs could possibly be better. The enjoyment I get from music is like a musical love affair.

Music has always been my comfort and my best friend. And it was my entertainment too. I had a bunch of those little vinyl 45s that I always looked forward to hearing. My daddy traveled out of town quite often and when he came home on the weekends, he would bring me the latest records that were out on the charts. I loved it!

I COULDN'T PLAY LIKE THEM

I didn't get out and play a lot with other children because most of the things they did were so visual. I had no way to see what was going on so I was pretty much left out; I was so limited.

I'm not saying that I never tried to do stuff with other kids. I'd go out on the playground and sort of join in. But you know, it just didn't work for me. And when I was home there weren't any children coming to my door saying, "Hey, Terri, you want to come, play?" I just didn't know how to adapt my blindness to what they were doing.

So, I guess I was kind of a loner growing up. When it came to being around other kids my age, I often turned to music-making instead. I found that I could play the game of musical notes whether I was alone or with others. I stayed indoors, I listened to music, and I played the piano probably every day. Oh, I had tea sets and dolls and the various things that little girls have. I liked them alright but the Lord gave me the gift of music which became my closest companion.

To me, music was magical. It soothed me; it pleased me; it took me to a deep place that sighted people might never get to find. It wasn't so much that I wasn't getting to do things with other kids. It's just that I loved music more. So, missing out on games for the sighted was alright with me.

I'm convinced that God put music deep into my heart. Nothing else gave me such a sense of belonging.

I know it was God's plan. And that special connection was a *life-saver*. In a world where everyone else had sight with which to enjoy life, I had a marvelous love through which I could see the unseen. It is the beauty of music that has carried me through and has given *me* a life to be enjoyed.

THE PIANO

Let me tell you how I came to play the piano. One day when I was just three years old, my grandmother's sister, Aunt Violet, had sat down to play the piano. It drew me and so I walked across the room to stand beside her. I wanted to be closer to that wonderful sound. The music just wrapped its arms around me and took me to a place of beautiful dreams that didn't need eyes to see. In the midst of my wonderment, and to my surprise, my Aunt picked me up and put me on her lap. Holding each of my hands in hers, she directed my little fingers, helping me to play a simple little melody on the keys.

That was it. The mold had been cast. The music shaped cavity in my heart became filled! I loved it!!

After a few minutes, my Aunt got up to visit with my grandmother. To her surprise, she heard me play that same simple little song right back to her with no mistakes as if I had played the song for years. Something inside me *turned on* that day. Music became a living language and a part of my inner person. It had been waiting there, ready to be stirred awake. And Aunt Violet brought it all to life at the keyboard.

A few years later--when I was seven years old--I heard the song *Fool Number One* by Brenda Lee on the radio. I went to the piano, sat down, and sang and played it with no mistakes. I'm sure no one knew what

33

I was going to do when I climbed onto the piano bench. But everyone in the house recognized the song and they all gathered around me to watch me sing and play. They were astonished at how I performed the whole song, perfectly. They were stunned and I was hooked!

I had already fallen deeply in love with the piano. It became a major part of my life. From then on, I wanted to play it all the time. God had given me a gift to build my life upon and now He was stirring it awake to be used. In later years I was told that I was born with perfect pitch so I guess that was just another confirmation for me. It was meant to be.

Performing for my family marked my beginnings; they were my very first audience. What I didn't know was that years later, that audience would grow into millions of fans who would attend my concerts and see my television appearances including one located on the other side of the world. It was 1983 when I was invited to tape a television show in New Zealand. Wow. I have traveled far and wide and God has amazed me by what He has done with my life. He has given me a gift and I have done my best to give it back to Him for His use and for His glory.

CHAPTER SEVEN
MY MUSICAL ROOTS

JOHN THOMAS KING

Yes, my roots in music go way back; long before *Somebody's Knockin'* was ever dreamed of. My family has been in music long before I was even born. My great-grandfather, John Thomas King, who was born in the 1800s, would travel from church to church each Sunday, singing and leading the music. Actually, he began what is now known as the "all day Gospel singing" in churches, and it's still going on today.

Great-Granddaddy King's love for Gospel music was passed down to many of us. For example, his daughter, (my grandmother, Effie King Gibbs), was from a family of ten children. She played the organ for over thirty-five years at her church, Marvin Methodist, of Martinez, Georgia.

I'll always remember Sunday dinners after church. They were like some huge celebration. My granddaddy, grandmother, aunts, uncles, and cousins would be there. After the table was cleared and the dishes were put away, we would all sit around and sing the old Gospel songs of love and faith. No one was ever in a hurry to leave. We'd have such a good time that before we knew it the sun would be going down and the afternoon would be gone, but we'd still be singing.

I'll never forget those days. They'll be in my memory forever. They were such happy times. I wish folks would still live that way today. It would make the world a nice place once again.

My daddy and one of his brothers worked hard on Granddaddy's dairy farm but they always made time for church on Sundays. Daddy and both of his brothers got together to sing at church functions if daddy wasn't working out of town. I used to play piano for these singing events and really enjoyed singing with my family. I wish Daddy was around today; I still miss him.

Others in my family have also been gifted and blessed with music. Ron Gibbs, one of my cousins, used to be with *Gabriel's Call,* a Southern Gospel group in Columbia, South Carolina. Today, he still sings and writes Christian music. Yes, music has been our tradition for many generations.

THE MUSIC TREE

When I think of how God has planted music in my heart, I think of how a tree begins and grows. Just like a tree with many leaves, my life is full of musical leaves. You see, God knew I needed something special. Especially when I was low and needed to be cheered up, or when I was unhappy. Music is what makes me smile when nothing else can.

I'd be very disappointed and upset if for some reason--and I hate to even speak or receive this--if I should lose my sense of hearing, I would lose more than just my ability to talk with people. I would also lose my music, and to me, that would be a loss almost greater than death.

If music were like water and it was to run out of my pores you could never drain me dry. It just couldn't happen. God has filled me so full of music that I'll never come to the end of it and I will never tire of it. I'm truly grateful to Him for that. He is the ultimate source of all good things.

ROOTS AND BRANCHES

I have listened to a lot of artists over the years that have shaped me, like Stevie Wonder, for example. But I would have to say that Ray Charles was one of my biggest influences. His music inspired and encouraged me to actually start singing professionally.

Ray was blind like I am, so I could really relate to him. And he was a true inspiration--so much so that I said to myself, "Hey, if he can do that, so can I." I decided right then that I wanted to be a singer too.

I related to Ray Charles for other reasons as well. First, he was born in Georgia, but his family was from Florida. Second, he also had his sight at birth but lost it accidentally when he was a child. Next, he learned to play the piano at the age of three, as did I. And, Ray died June 10th, just five days before my birthday. So, we had several similarities between us.

His approach was to mix several musical genres together to create his unique style. He blended blues, jazz, gospel, and country, which is sort of what I did when I was starting out.

Frank Sinatra called Ray Charles "the only true genius in show business." Another well-known singer, Billy Joel said, "This may sound like sacrilege but I think Ray Charles was more important than Elvis Presley to the music world."

As important as he was to the industry, I often said, "If Ray Charles had ever become saved, I wouldn't have been able to stand it. His singing for Jesus would have been "off the chain" for me! My heart was sad, though, because I hadn't heard whether he had accepted the Lord. It was just one of those things that stuck in my mind, and I had a hard time getting away from it.

But God is so good! One night I found some hope. I was listening to a Christian TV program, and I felt Jesus very near to me. As I fell asleep, I could hear Scripture being read. Later, in the middle of the night, I woke up and heard a woman talking about Ray Charles. She said he had told her he was mad at God because God took his mother at such a young age. She said, "Ray, the Lord did not take your mother; He received her. You can receive Jesus right here and you'll see your momma again when *you* get to heaven."

I was so encouraged that God woke me up just at the right moment to hear that lady speak to Ray about Jesus. If I had woken up two minutes later, I would have missed it. Jesus cares about all of our concerns and nothing is too big or too small to ask of Him. And what God has done for me, He will do for you.

My concern for Ray Charles was a matter of prayer, and the Lord answered my prayer in such a special way. Jesus comforted me by letting me know Ray had heard the truth and became saved. I surely look forward to hearing him, and singing with him in that heavenly choir one day!

CHAPTER EIGHT
GEORGIA ON MY MIND

MY BLESSED HOME

I've appreciated the many blessings I've had growing up. My home life was stable and that meant staying in familiar schools through the years. A friend of mine told me her family moved so often that she went to fifteen different schools in twelve years. She must have missed out on a lot because of constantly trying to adjust.

I mentioned earlier that we lived with my daddy's parents until I was four years old. They owned a lot of land just off of Belair Road. The house was on a dirt road about twenty miles from downtown Augusta. Some folks would call that *living in the sticks.* But that's alright with me. It was *countrified* and I make no bones about it.

I loved staying with my grandparents. For one thing, they had a piano in the house. I could go to that piano and talk to it about all of my griefs and triumphs. When I was eleven, my grandmother bought me my own piano which I still have today. It sits in my living room and I still enjoy playing it. It comforts me. Actually, it is really priceless to me *because* it came from Grandmother.

As a young girl living on the farm, I used to enjoy going into town when the chance arose. It was a *fair piece* to get there as we say here in the South. Belair Road was a winding dirt road through endless plats of farmland. It was far from the hub-bub of things so for me, those trips were special. Today, we think nothing of riding twenty or thirty minutes to go somewhere.

Much has changed. It's still called Belair Road, but it's also Exit 194 that comes off of Interstate 20 which passes east and west through the northern edge of Augusta. The Belair Road area has become so absorbed by industry and commercialism that the whole area is filled with miles and miles of businesses. It has grown seamlessly into the city of Augusta, although it's still its own individual town. The name eventually changed from Belair to the City of Grovetown. It has become a fast-growing and vibrant offshoot of Augusta.

In 1958, the population of Augusta was about 40,000 people but today there are one-quarter million people who call Augusta their home. That makes it the second largest city in Georgia, covering over three hundred square miles. Only Atlanta, the state capital, is larger with an inner-city population of one half million (and over five and a half million in the metropolitan area). To me, Grovetown will always be good-old, small-town, southern-country living, and the place where I grew up.

DREAMING ABOUT *THE BELL*

One of my favorite places in Augusta is the Bell Auditorium. It's a large building built specifically for entertainment and variety shows. Around here we affectionately call it *the Bell.* Some of the biggest events in show business have headlined there: country singers, ballet performances, stage plays, and other worldwide attractions. They say there isn't a bad seat in the house and the reclining leather chairs are a big plus for comfort.

As a young girl, I dreamed of singing at the Bell. I thought it would be wonderful! Performing music was something I was already doing, so in my mind, it was possible.

By the time I was six years old I was singing at church. A couple of years later I remember being asked to sing at our Bible school program. I was eight then, in third grade. It was June of 1962. That same year I was asked to sing in front of my classmates at school. I stood there and sang an old Beatles song: *Eight Days a Week*. You know, when you're young you just don't have any guardrails up.

Several times, I was asked to sing in front of the school assembly. It was during one of those times that my English teacher, Miss Elsie Snyder, said to me, "Terri, you are going to make it big someday and you are going to be famous." It was like she prophesied over me. Well, she hadn't, but she had.

What I mean is, when we speak, we often prophesy or claim our future and we don't even know it. Sometimes the power of words being spoken into our lives can make such an impression that they begin to form our direction. We don't realize it but we can say something good, or we can say something not so good. As we grow older, we then reap what we've sown by the words of our mouth. So, we ought to be careful about what we say or declare. Without intending to, we may point our lives in the direction of our words.

Looking back, I must say Miss Snyder was one of my biggest encouragers in life. Because of her, I began to have the faith I needed to believe. I planned to hang onto my dream of singing at the Bell one day. But at that young age, I'd have to wait quite a while to see if it would really happen. I thought, "I'll just have to believe God; I'll just have to wait upon Him to show me how it will all come to pass."

SOMEWHERE OVER THE RAINBOW

Throughout my life, I've always had opportunities to sing or play. I'll always remember Miss Lucky, my fourth-grade teacher. Miss Lucky had taught us the song, *Somewhere Over the Rainbow.* Just before we broke for lunch one day, she asked me to sing the song in front of the class.

Often times as a junior and senior at Butler High School, I was asked to play the piano for special assemblies. I was also in Girls' Chorus in grade eleven and in Advanced Chorus in grade twelve. God was bringing me one opportunity after another. Without a doubt, I can look back and see how God was preparing me for a future in music.

People often say, "Seeing is believing". As a blind person I say, "Believing is seeing." I saw music in my future and believed God would do His part. I had much hope for the future and waited for the Lord to bring things to pass.

There's a wonderful verse in the book of Matthew. Jesus said, **". . . if you have faith as small as a mustard seed . . . Nothing will be impossible for you,"** (Matthew 17:20; NIV).

A mustard seed is so small you can hardly see it. That sounds like the kind of faith I had! But it was enough. I had the assurance that my tiny faith would be accepted by the Lord; then He'd take my life and do things with it that would glorify Him. Through His power, I would accomplish more than I could ever imagine. While I waited to see where faith would take me I continued to sing and play every chance I had. And what a great adventure it was.

The Bible says, **"Where there is no vision, the people perish,"** (Proverbs 29:18; KJV). I didn't want my vision to perish. So, I kept going forward to the best of my ability.

I know kids have all kinds of dreams that usually just fade away. But I really did want to sing at the Bell and beyond. To me it was real; I could see it before me; I could envision it. When Country singers came to Augusta, Momma would take me to see their shows. That kept my hopes alive through my younger years.

Yes, it was just as simple as that! I wanted to spend my life performing music and I believed it would happen because I felt God was on my side. I wasn't going to give up, and I didn't. God worked through other people and arranged things and circumstances. In due time, everything did begin to bloom just like I had wished.

CHAPTER NINE
SEEING WITHOUT SIGHT

THANKS TO MOMMA ONCE AGAIN

I had quite a taste for adventure growing up. It was good that my parents raised me to be independent so I could do things for myself. When I was little, I learned to ride a tricycle in our carport. There were no walls, just the concrete slab. So once in a while, I'd slip off the edge and fall. But I always got up and went at it again.

Later, I learned to ride a bicycle all by myself. That caused me to want to go further than my yard, so I would go riding with my cousin. I would listen to the noise of her wheels as they rolled along the ground. I would follow that sound so I could know where to go. I had a great time at it too. Riding a bicycle was something I could do with the other kids. What a thrill!

Another favorite pass time of mine was reading. I still like to read today. I learned how to read Braille when I was only five years old. That was before I had started school. By the time I settled in school I was reading everything I could get a hold of.

I so appreciate the fact that Momma learned the Braille system along with me. She worked hard at it so that later on, she could help me with my homework assignments. I have to say, "Thanks Momma for helping me. Because of you and Aunt Helen, I brought home mostly A's and B's. Without your help, I may never have had those kinds of scores at graduation. Thank you so much!"

THE BOOKS WEIGHED A TON!

I don't know if any of you have ever seen or examined a Braille book. Compared to printed books, Braille books are much larger because of the pages and pages of raised dots they contain.

All through the years, I had to carry Braille books around as I went to my classes and traveled back and forth to and from school. Those books weighed a ton!

I still have many Braille books today. The one I treasure most is my Bible. Well, it's actually a set of books and I have them right here beside my bed. As my fingers dance across the pages at night drawing me closer to God through His words, I find they're always there to comfort me. I don't need a light on to see what the pages are saying. I can see God's encouraging words through my fingertips; they go deep into my heart and carry me to sleep. What a blessing.

TRANSITIONS

Getting back to my school days, there was a man named John Pierce Blanchard who was born in Columbia County. He taught school for several years and later became Superintendent of Schools, a position he held for three decades.

While he was Superintendent, he started a special program in Augusta for students with disabilities. As I mentioned earlier, disabled and visually impaired students like myself would usually have to go to Macon, Georgia for their education. Instead, I was integrated with sighted students because of this program, and that opportunity greatly broadened my horizons. Culturally speaking, it gave me a big advantage because I learned how to live in the *real* world rather than being isolated in a school for the blind. Being mixed in with people who could see gave me a much better grasp of normal life.

I started first grade at Evans School. For second grade I went to Wilkinson Gardens School in Richmond County, although I still lived in Columbia County. And though I was enrolled in the special needs program, I spent time in regular classes with sighted children as well. The teachers in those classes would give me extra help with whatever I was working on.

Then I went to the brand-new school in Windsor Springs. And later in 1967, I transferred back to Columbia County.

Finally, in 1970 I moved on to Butler High school in Richmond County for tenth grade where I later graduated.

A FAITHFUL FRIEND

There were many things to encourage me through the years. I had pass-times like reading or being with special girlfriends who played with me and brought enjoyment my way. I had great parents and family and lots of love in our home.

Of course, music was my special friend. I often confessed what was in my heart to my piano through the keys and it would never ask questions, argue, or criticize. God is so good to His children and He's proved that to me by giving me so many blessings.

Maybe there are times when you need someone to lean on. If so, God is always available to listen and help. There's a song by Gordon Jensen called, *He's As Close As The Mention Of His Name.* Many times, I've called on His name and He's always been right there. If you have a need but you feel that no one cares, just know that the Lord truly cares for you.

Try having a serious heart to heart talk with God. Even as faithful as my piano was, God was many times more faithful to me. I promise you God will always listen to you; He will never let you down or turn you away. Why not try Him and see?

CHAPTER TEN
NEW HORIZONS IN MUSIC

RADIO-LAND

When I was sixteen years old, there was a little 45 RPM record label by the name of Starlight Enterprises. They had hooked up with WGUS radio, 102.3 FM, in Augusta and first signed on the air in late 1967. It was called Big Gus Country Radio.

From time to time the station would hold singing contests and through the use of Starlight Enterprises they would put the winner on the radio and create a 45 RPM recording of their song. I was fortunate enough to have made a recording with the label. Because of that, I was chosen to sing at the Bell! Can you imagine?!

All this time I thought of how exciting it would be if it could really happen someday. Now it was real! I was *actually* going to sing at the Bell Auditorium! Something was starting to happen.

BILL ANDERSON

In 1970, the door to my dreams opened even wider. Country music star Bill Anderson was performing at the Bell Auditorium. He had such a smooth, soft voice that he earned the nickname *Whispering Bill*. One of Anderson's big hits, *City Lights,* was said to have been written overlooking Augusta, Georgia. To be fair, I've also heard that he wrote it while he was in Commerce, Georgia, (several miles from here).

It so happened that because of my recording sessions with WGUS Radio, I was asked if I wanted to open for him.

I thought, "What? Me? Open for Bill Anderson? Would I? *Yes! Of course, I would!*" It was another dream coming true. Not only was he a Country music star but he was also the producer of a talent show called *You Can Be a Star*, hosted by fellow Grand Ole Opry member Jim Ed Brown.

As the day of my performance drew near, I couldn't tell you how excited I was. I was going to sing at the Bell. Amazing! And I was only sixteen. I had never been in front of that many people before but I was really looking forward to it.

Finally, the day came and it was time. I walked on stage and sang the song, *A Stranger in My Place.* It was an Anne Murray song; they said I brought the house down. Who could have guessed that? I was beside myself! My big dream was coming to pass and I knew God had to be in it.

Two years later I was back at the Bell. It was 1972 and graduation ceremonies were being held there for Butler High School. I was so proud to walk across that stage to receive my diploma. I worked hard for my grades. I felt so blessed.

Ten years later Butler High School expanded. They added a new music building to their campus. When it was completed on March 23, 1983, the Board of Education of Richmond County dedicated the new building as follows: In honor of Miss Terri Gibbs, 1972 Butler graduate and Country music star. How about that!

Yes, they named it after that little baby girl born in Miami, Florida; the one that was not predicted to live. People think so highly of themselves to think they can outguess God or know His plans. Here was proof that God knows more than doctors and everybody. And He can certainly make little girls' dreams come true. His ways are much higher than our ways, aren't they?

WIKIPEDIA'S ARTICLE ABOUT MISS TERRI GIBBS

On March 23, 1983, the new music complex at Butler High School was named the Terri Gibbs Music Center in honor of Country and Gospel singer Terri Gibbs, a 1972 Butler High graduate. At the dedicatory service, Gibbs played the piano and sang the state song, "Georgia on My Mind." Terri, blind from birth, was a resident of Columbia County and was allowed to attend Butler High School because Butler offered a special education program for handicapped students. The center is an impressive structure dedicated to developing the musical talents of students. At one end of the building is a large chorus rehearsal room, and at the other end is a large room for rehearsing Butler High's band. Between these anchor rooms are several individual practice rooms and individual offices for the band and choral directors.

--Wikipedia

CHAPTER ELEVEN
NASHVILLE AND THE MUSIC WORLD

MEETING CHET ATKINS!

In April of 1972, Chet Atkins came to town along with Floyd Cramer and Boots Randolph to do a concert at the Bell Auditorium. At that time Millard Beckum was the mayor of Augusta. He arranged for me to meet Atkins, one on one, person to person.

I thought, "C'mon! Chet Atkins? Are you kidding me?" But he wasn't kidding. I got to go back-stage to meet him. I was on pins and needles. Wow! This was as good as it gets!

Incidently, Floyd Cramer had played piano for Elvis Presley, Brenda Lee, Patsy Cline, Jim Reeves, Eddy Arnold, Roy Orbison, the Everly Brothers and many others. He became famous for his unusual piano playing style.

And Boots Randolph played saxophone on records for Roy Orbison, Jerry Lee Lewis, Brenda Lee, REO Speedwagon, Al Hirt and Chet Atkins as well as many others. Both of them were music giants in Nashville and here I was in the midst of it all.

So, I met with Atkins. He talked with me, encouraged me, and asked me to send him a tape so he could hear my voice. I was hoping he would ask me to audition right then, and was disappointed that he didn't. I had heard so many stories about people who had also sent their tapes to Nashville without any response.

Later on, when I had gained more experience, I realized that performers can't just stop everything to listen to someone sing. Never-the-less I remember putting together a collection of some of my original compositions plus a few of my favorite country songs and sent them anyway.

Our meeting came and went. Then later that year, my birthday came along on June 15th. I turned eighteen and Momma surprised me with a marvelous birthday present; a shopping trip! We were getting ready to go shop when the phone rang. I answered it and a voice said, "Hi Terri, this is Chet Atkins."

Momma knew something was wrong because she said my face went as white as a sheet. I thought surely someone was playing a trick on me, but I knew it was for real because I remembered his voice.

Chet said he wanted me to come to Nashville to meet some of the record company executives who had heard my tape. I was ready to leave right then and I was so excited. Now *that* was quite a birthday present!

Later, when I met the record people Chet was hoping to secure a record deal for me but was told my voice wasn't quite mature enough yet. They thought I had great potential and Chet told me to keep singing and writing and not give up. He said I had a gift that was going to take me somewhere.

When they told me that, I remembered Miss Snyder's words seven years earlier when she said, "Terri, you are going to make it big someday."

I GET TO CUT A RECORD
I began making lots of tapes and continued to send them off to Nashville. Back then we used reel-to-reel recorders and tapes which were larger than cassettes. When cassettes finally came out a few years later they were more accessible and easier to use.

I remember picking out one particular tape and sending it to a guy named Jim Owen. He liked what he heard. Now, he had a few of his own songs but his style was that of a Hank Williams imitator. He also produced those 45 RPM records for Starlight Enterprises. So, with his help, we made a 45-record called, *Let It Shine*. I think it was September of 1971. I don't know how many records I sold but I do remember selling them during my senior year at Butler High.

Owen and I actually wrote a song together that ended up on an album done by Jim Ed Brown. It was called, *It's That Time of the Night,* and the song title was, *After Dark.* At that time Jim Owen was working at a song publishing company in Nashville which used a lot of country singers, so he accepted some of my original songs.

In 1973 I was in College in Augusta. I sang back-up for my cousin, Ron Gibbs, and his band, The Sound Dimensions. Also, for about a year--on Saturdays and many weeknights--I played music in the upstairs lounge at the Continental Hotel, across the street from the Augusta Airport.

In 1974 Owen wanted to try to get me a recording deal. Of course, I was excited and I told him that I was really interested, but it didn't happen just then. I was patient, though. I stayed busy singing everywhere and anywhere I could get an engagement.

IS THERE A DOCTOR IN THE HOUSE

I had another long run from October of 1978 through February of 1981. I sang and played piano at the Steak and Ale Restaurant in Augusta, Georgia. A lot of people remember me from back then. I played five nights a week and played some forty to fifty songs a night. Sometimes I worked until one o'clock in the morning.

Doctor Paul Thaxton and his wife came to eat there all the time. His wife's name was also Terri. They would often come in just to sit and listen to me sing. One evening Doctor Paul said, "Young lady, you need to be singing in Nashville. I think we might be able to help you do that. So if you ever decide to, let me know. I'll be glad to help you out."

It had been five years since I had made tapes and now suddenly, I had another opportunity. So, I went ahead with it. And I accepted Doctor Thaxton's offer to help. He put up the money for me to make a tape and it was sent to the same company Jim Owen had previously worked with when trying to get me a recording deal. I was overwhelmed with appreciation and I was grateful for another chance to go forward with my music.

CHAPTER TWELVE
RUBBING SHOULDERS WITH THE STARS

CALLED TO NASHVILLE
There was a man in Nashville by the name of Ed Penney. He was a song writer who worked for a publishing company. His role was to pitch songs to artists so that he could bring artists and songs together. He wanted to get good Country artists recorded, just like Jim Owen had been doing.

Ed Penney came across a tape I had made. It was one that Jim Owen and I had worked on previously. After listening to the tape, Mr. Penny was interested in me and wanted to know who I was. All anyone could remember at the time was that I was a blind girl from Georgia. I sent another tape to this company because I hoped they might remember me and give me some assistance. This tape was the one I had made with the help of Paul Thaxton. Penny was very interested at this point, especially in my voice because he wanted to become a record producer.

To my surprise, Ed Penny contacted me and then came to Augusta to the Steak and Ale where I was performing at the time. He suggested that I come to Nashville to make a demo tape.

So, we made the tape and Ed Penny presented it to Jim Foglesong who was the President of MCA records. Ed hoped Jim would sign me to MCA and allow Ed to be my producer.

ON MY WAY TO A HIT SONG
Let me tell you a bit about MCA's Jim Foglesong. He was an executive music producer in Nashville from the 1950s through the late 1990s. Jim began his career

in the industry with the Columbia Records' label in 1951, transferring 78 RPM records to LPs. During his coming-up years, he also sang in quartets and trios on local radio shows from his teens into his young adult years.

Over the next 20 years, he worked for RCA-Victor. He then moved to Nashville in 1970 to work for Dot Records. He was named president of Dot Records in 1973 and changed the company's vision from Pop music to Country music. That shift gave many singers the opportunity to be heard and many became Country music stars.

Jim Foglesong helped lay the foundation for the 1990s *boom* in Country music. As president of Capitol, Dot, ABC, and MCA Records, he signed popular artists such as Barbara Mandrell, Don Williams, Garth Brooks, Donna Fargo, Reba McEntire, the Oak Ridge Boys, Tanya Tucker, Sawyer Brown and George Strait. He was one of the most influential persons in the music industry.

Jim Fogelsong promoted a lot of music. His picks won 46 Grammys, and CMA and ACM awards, and in 2004 he was inducted into the Country Music Hall of Fame. I could see I had pretty strong leadership behind me with someone like Fogelsong at the helm. I'll always be thankful to him for believing in me and helping my career.

So, I was signed by MCA in February of 1980. The first recording session was completed in June of that year. They wanted me to record six songs and said, "If you have a hit, we'll let you do a whole album." I was really excited.

Just imagine! Me, a little blind country girl from Georgia was going to sign a recording contract with MCA, one of the largest recording companies in the world. And they wanted *me*. I was amazed!

SUCCESS!

When we started the project, I recorded some of Ed Penny's own compositions, one of which was, *Somebody's Knockin'* that he co-wrote with Jerry Gillespie.

They had actually wanted to release the B side first, which was a song called, *Some Days It Rains All Night Long.* But Ed talked them into releasing *Somebody's Knockin'* instead. In turn, he promised he would call the radio stations and do all the promotion. They finally agreed and *Somebody's Knockin'* was released August 21st, 1980. I was on my way.

The single, *Somebody's Knockin'*, was so successful that it made it to number eight on the U.S. Billboard Hot Country Singles, and then crossed over to the Pop charts and made it to number thirteen. It also reached number three on the U.S. Billboard Hot Adult Contemporary Charts and number two on the Canadian RPM Country charts. Those were great stats; the song created quite a stir

A VERY SPECIAL NIGHT!

It was April of 1981. The Academy of Country Music Awards was in full swing. That awesome night had finally arrived and I could hardly believe I was there, standing backstage as nervous as a cat. I was waiting to see who would get the award for Top New Female Vocalist of the Year. I was a nominee in the running with Reba McEntire, Sissy Spacek, Kim Carnes, and Sylvia, who made it to the number one spot with her big hit, *Nobody.* That was pretty tough competition, especially since I was an unknown.

The audience was packed for the occasion and there were probably millions watching on television. Suddenly everything was quiet and I knew this was the moment of truth. Who would get the award? Who would be the winner? Surely not me. The waiting was driving me crazy. I was one of five people nominated that night, so what chance did I have? Just a few more minutes and I would know.

Standing behind the curtains, I knew Momma was sitting up front in the audience where she could see me. Daddy was working out of town that night and couldn't make it to the awards but I was sure he would be watching it on TV.

I thought about the others who were nominated that evening, and I knew they were all very good. I said to myself, "Reba McEntire is already a legend so what chance do I have against her? I've only been around for about eight months, so I'm a just a newcomer. Surely one of them will get it."

Kim Carnes was right up there too with her song, *Don't Fall in Love with a Dreamer.* She sang that as a duet with Kenny Rogers which made it to number one on the charts.

Sissy Spacek's *Coal Miner's Daughter* was also huge. It had already won her an Oscar for the movie. In that movie, she sang Loretta Lynn's hit song by the same name and it earned a Grammy nomination.

So here I was an upstart. I knew a lot of people were talking about my song and were listening to it on the radio. I knew that record sales were up. Stores had sold thousands of copies of it. So, I guess I had a shot at it but I'd have to wait and see.

AND THE WINNER IS . . .

Finally, the envelope was in hand. Someone opened it and then I heard the announcement. "And the winner is . . . Miss Terri Gibbs!" I couldn't believe it! That was the biggest surprise of my life. I could have passed out right there. I had won the Academy of Country Music's New Female Vocalist Award. It became a life-changing moment. My legs were shaking, my head was spinning and I didn't know if I could get my next breath.

My manager, Ed Penney, took me by the arm and led me to the center of the stage. The audience must have been glad too because they busted loose into wild applause. I remember walking onto the platform and thinking that Momma was probably crying. It sure meant a lot to have her there that wonderful night.

After a moment or two I heard a rustling noise coming from the floor of the auditorium and somehow, I just knew they were giving me a standing ovation. I didn't know what to think or what to do. I had butterflies and goose-bumps. I was the winner! I was stunned and amazed!

God blessed me so. In October of that year, I also won the very first Horizon Award ever presented by the Country Music Association. Later on, they changed the name to the New Artist Award.

Then in 1982, I received a Grammy nomination for Best Country Song of the year.

Other artists who recorded Ed Penny's songs were Glen Campbell, Barbara Mandrell, Jerry Lee Lewis, Hank Williams, Jr., Eddy Arnold, and Anne Murray. But of course, I'm glad that Ed produced *Somebody's Knockin'* with me in mind.

Looking back on it now, I see that it was such a "God thing." I didn't even realize that Ed Penny had inquired about me, yet the Lord prompted me to send a tape. It was truly a Cinderella story!

CHAPTER THIRTEEN
FAME, FRIENDS, AND FAITH

A FAMOUS MOMENT

After the show, my momma joined me. She told me the camera had focused in on a close up of her as tears were streaming down her face. She was worried people would see that her mascara was ruined. She said, "I tried to turn away from the camera but every time I turned away from one camera, there was another one in my face."

Of course, Momma's story made me laugh. She added later that when she got back home to Grovetown after the awards show she couldn't go anywhere without someone saying, "Hey Betty, I saw you crying on TV." I still think it's funny!

SAYING GOODBYE TO FRIENDS

Let me share a bit more about my friends, Jim Foglesong and Chet Atkins. They were a big part of my life and I'm so grateful for our ties.

Jim Foglesong was a World War II veteran of the United States Army and a graduate of the Eastman School of Music in Rochester, New York. After many years in the recording industry, he retired and became head of the Music Business Department of Trevecca Nazarene University in Nashville, a Christian college which is still active today. Jim also taught a Business of Music class at Vanderbilt University.

Jim Foglesong died on July 9, 2013, at the age of 90. Losing him was a great loss for me and for the music world. I'm so thankful for the short time that I knew him and I'll never forget the kind help he gave me in getting my career started. He was truly

63

instrumental in the 1981 hit song, *Somebody's Knockin'*. He was also a wonderful Christian man and will always have a place in my heart.

BYE BYE TO CHET ATKINS

And about Chet Atkins. He was so sweet; he called to congratulate me on the success of *Somebody's Knockin'.* At the same time, he asked me to go to lunch with him, but he said, "Girl, you better not order just a hamburger!"

We had a nice lunch and a nice long talk. To be honest, I was in awe of him so it was quite special when he asked me to come to his house to play piano with him while he played the guitar. I wish I had taken him up on the offer. I have never considered myself a keyboardist because of my having learned to play by ear. But Chet Atkins was also self-taught on the guitar so he understood where I was coming from.

Chet rose to great heights on his instrument. He had actually learned the song *Somebody's Knockin'* and recorded it as an instrumental. That meant so much to me.

Chet Atkins--well known in Nashville and throughout the Country Music industry as "Mr. Guitar"--has also left this earthly life. He passed away November 30, 2001, at the age of seventy-seven. And I should mention that Reverend Paul Baggett was known to have led Chet Atkins to salvation through Christ. It's so wonderful that he is living out his heavenly life with the Lord Jesus. Because of that, I know I'll see Chet again one day.

Now think about this: when I get to heaven and I catch up with him and his heavenly guitar, I'll get to play the piano with him. Imagine me and Chet doing music together. Won't that be terrific? We'll probably spend the first couple of hundred years praising and worshiping the Lord. I'm sure of it . . . and even that amount of time won't be long enough to sing honors to our great God. He is so worthy to be praised.

JUST THANKFUL

I'm thankful for so many things like having the parents that I did. But I have to point to my greatest help once again. It was God Himself who opened the way for me to become a professional entertainer. He was "the wind beneath my wings". He continually drove me forward and strengthened me when I needed it. And there were plenty of times when I needed it, believe me.

I had moments of self-doubt. I had periods of loneliness when traveling far from home. That was hard to do. And there were times when I was just plain tired. But I knew I could always turn to God's faithfulness to pull me through.

ENCOURAGING OTHERS

Of course, being blind has had its setbacks and I've had to be determined, daily, to not let it get the better of me. Every new day has new challenges but each day is also an opportunity to learn more and become a more productive individual in spite of what I have to live with.

I have to keep seeing myself as not being different from others. In fact, I even have advantages over sighted people in some respects. I say that because some of my other senses have become more finely tuned. My keen sense of hearing, for example, has given me the opportunity to learn new skills which I might not have had the chance to do otherwise.

I really hope my life has been an example for those without physical sight. And I hope I have encouraged sighted people with or without other disabilities as well. We all need to be encouraged to not give up in the midst of our struggles.

I hope you use every ability God has given you to do the very best you can. My wish for you is that you accomplish all you have ever dreamed of doing. And may your wishes come true.

SON-LIGHT

Dreams are the stuff life is made of. Someone once said, "When you cease to dream you cease to live." So, what do I still dream about? Well, I dream about heaven all the time. It's going to be fabulous! I'll get to see butterflies and flowers, the beauty of God's creation, and many other marvels. I get goose-bumps just thinking about it.

There's something else I'm looking forward to. For the first time ever, I'll get to see my own family and friends. I can't begin to describe what that'll be like.

Most importantly, beyond all else I've talked about, I'll get to see the One Who makes eternal life possible. He is the One who invites each of us to journey with Him in this life and the life to come. He is Jesus, and He will be the *first* thing I'll see. I'll be able to look at Jesus with a clear vision and what a marvelous sight He will be. Like the song says, I can only imagine.

While I have never seen the effects of sunlight that define shapes and colors, from the moment I enter heaven I'll never be in the shadows again. Once I pass through those pearly gates the night will cease and the day will reign for eternity.

The light of Jesus Who is called the Lamb and the Son of God--His presence alone will light all of Heaven. He will be our "Son-light", and we will bathe in His presence for all eternity. We'll walk with Him and talk with Him and sing songs of praise to Him forever more. I am so looking forward to that day!

CHAPTER FOURTEEN
A PLACE CALLED HOME

ON THE ROAD

It was because *Somebody's Knockin'* had climbed up so many popular charts, that the door opened wide for me to go on the road. For the next few years beginning May of 1981 I traveled everywhere, to open for artists such as Alabama and George Jones.

I was becoming pretty well known and I started getting a lot of interviews. People wanted to know how the song was changing my life. Once a lady asked me, "Now that you're becoming famous, what's something you'd like to do?" I told her I'd like to have a nice home.

I guess the folks in the real estate world were really paying attention that day. Before I knew it I had visits from all kinds of salespeople wanting me to buy a house.

CHAMBLIN ROAD

It wasn't something I was ready to do right then, but there was an agent from Grovetown who said he had a very special house to show me on Chamblin Road. I didn't really want to go and see it but I went anyway.

When I got there and saw the house, I fell in love with it. It was huge and it was beautiful. It had six bedrooms and five and a half baths. That was a lot of room for a single person but I hoped to marry one day and raise my family there.

I was also attracted to the house because as an avid reader, many of the characters in the books I read always lived in large homes and I always imagined myself in a home like that. I wasn't sure if I should buy it but since I could afford it, I decided to go ahead. When I moved in, I realized how that living space really was! A person could easily get lost there.

THEY SACRIFICED FOR ME

So, I bought my first house, but my life was very busy. I was flying back and forth to and from Nashville, working and traveling with my band so I didn't get to spend a lot of time there. With all the square feet that big house had, I was glad when Momma and Daddy moved in with me. They took care of things when I was gone, and when I was home, I enjoyed being with them more than I can tell you.

For one thing, I was glad to finally have something to give back to them. They gave up a lot to raise me. They helped me in more ways than I can describe. I didn't know how I could ever repay them but now my chance had come. I could finally share the good life with them. My heart was full.

BIGGER THAN A BREAD-BOX!

My Chamblin Road house was definitely bigger than a bread-box! I went from a 720 square foot mobile home to a 6800 square foot estate!! It was a lot to take care of but it was a blessing from God; yes, I had come a long way since my days at the Bell Auditorium.

Some of my fondest memories were coming home to my wonderful house after being on the road. I loved having the time to relax in beautiful surroundings or maybe sit on the deck and unwind.

Another thing I loved about that house was the cabana out back. It was next to the swimming pool. I didn't swim but I enjoyed the water very much so I bought a pair of adult size water-wings and I used them to float around in the water all day. We had several family get-togethers there too. We would gather around for food and fun and spend the afternoons lying out in the sun.

Sometimes we would have friends come over for what you might call pool parties. We'd cook out all day and enjoy the starlit sky in the evenings when the sun went down. Those evenings were so pleasant.

It reminds of an old song written in 1954--the same year I was born--called *Fly Me to the Moon*. It was sung by the greats like Tony Bennett, Frank Sinatra, and Nat King Cole. There's a line in the song that says. "Fly me to the moon and let me play among the stars." Those evenings were actually like playing among the stars and having the moon--which I have never seen--right there within my reach. That's how those nights made me feel.

WHAT COULD BE MISSING?

Those old memories were sort of mystical and magic-like. I was living the high life like the rest of the Nashville/Hollywood folks. It only lasted for a few of years but I thought the rest of my life would be equally as perfect.

I found that there's a difference between joy and fun. Life had become a lot of fun. There was all the traveling, meeting famous people, going to foreign countries, and being recognized and known wherever I went. Living the big dream was fun. It's what I envisioned when Miss Snyder spoke to me that day long ago.

In the back of my mind, though, I wondered if I was handling things well. Maybe I was running ahead of God or leaving Him out altogether. When I saw that all of the fun was coming from my fame and fortune, I also knew it wasn't going to last forever. It could all change over-night. What if sadness came to knock on my door? Well, it kind of did.

Suddenly I needed more than glitz. I needed peace in my life but that was getting harder to find. Having all the things in the world couldn't fix that for me. So, what was missing? There I was, in the middle of a big shiny world . . . but I was lonely.

CHAPTER FIFTEEN
THE WORLD OF TELEVISION

AMERICAN BANDSTAND

Back in the day, I remember appearing on American Bandstand with Dick Clark. He was one of the nicest people you could ever want to meet. I was at the piano while their theme song was playing; it was a rock and roll number. As it faded out Dick Clark slid in next to me on the bench.

He said, "That isn't Country music!" He said it for my benefit because right behind that he said, "They call you a Country artist but you make music that appeals to everyone. How long have you been at it?"

I told him, "A l-o-o-o-n-g time. I started when I was three years old."

"How did you ever get started in music?"

I told him about beginning on the piano at three and how I fell in love with it.

"Earlier we were talking about perfect pitch. Would you explain that to those of us who don't understand what that means?"

So, I explained how some people can name a note just by hearing it in the air, without having a reference like a piano or an instrument to rely on.

Then he asked me what I was going to sing. I said the song was called *I Want to Be Around to Pick Up the Pieces.*

"Who did that song?"

"Why Tony Bennett of course!"

Jokingly he said, "You aren't old enough to remember him! You're lying! You can't be that old!"

Yes, Dick Clark was a gem. He was also known as "the world's oldest living teenager". I guess I would say he was like Champagne. He was sweet and bubbly and a real joy to know.

American Bandstand had made an early impression on me. I remember listening to it as a child. In fact, one of the programs I heard was an episode that featured Stevie Wonder. He sang the song, *Fingertips,* and played harmonica on it too. He was only thirteen years old at the time and I'll never forget it. Now all these years later, here I was on the show. You never know where life's going to take you. I never dreamed I'd be up there myself one day.

If you would like, you can see the video of that American Bandstand episode at the following website. I think you'd enjoy seeing the whole interview because Dick Clark was such a wonderful person to listen to. Here's the web address:

https://www.youtube.com/watch?v=128srXCw4wo

OTHER MEMORABLE SHOWS

Besides the thrill of being on the American Bandstand, I've sung with Barbara Mandrell, on the Barbara Mandrell show. One of the songs we did was, *Dream Lover.* I remember the fun we had doing that.

I've also appeared on Glenn Campbell's TV show, and on *Solid Gold* with Dionne Warwick, the Merv Griffin Show, the John Davidson Show, the Grand Ole Opry, as well as *Good Morning America* on the ABC network.

Then I've sung at Madison Square Garden. And I was honored when George Jones took me on tour with them in about 1982. I was blessed to perform in London, England with Mel Tillis. And I was so very glad to have had the chance to sing for our military troops in Germany in 1984.

74

I've sung in just about every state in the Union and have greatly appreciated the many opportunities given to me. As I look back on my life, I confess I've had some great experiences. I went from singing back-up in a band and playing at the Continental Hotel at the age of nineteen, to being invited to appear on some of the most popular TV shows of the day. I am blessed.

The bright lights of the entertainment world were exciting and I found out that dreams do come true. But glamor is only a small part of a fulfilled life. I still had an emptiness that I couldn't seem to fill. There had to be more to life than this, but what could it be?

CHAPTER SIXTEEN
GOD CAUGHT UP TO ME

JOY IN A BOOKSTORE

While there were plenty of thrills for this Georgia gal, the biggest reward of all came in November of 1986. While in Nashville I learned that a lot of famous Country singers were going to a particular prayer meeting, held regularly in the back room of the Koinonia Christian Bookstore. I decided I would go. I attended at times before, just to enjoy the live Christian music.

Everyone would sing together; some brought guitars to add to the mix. And once again, I was amazed to be with such talented people as Barbara Fairchild, Jeanie C. Riley, Rickie Scaggs, and Connie Smith. I listened to each of them on the radio when I was little. Now, here they were right in front of me. It was interesting to be there and see what was going on. I found myself drawn to being like them.

We had times of sharing too. We'd talk about our lives and we'd share our special prayer needs with one another. It was just good old Christian fellowship at its best.

I remember going to a particular meeting that I almost missed because I hadn't slept very well the night before. I had been worrying about my decision to change over to Christian music. I was also concerned about my ability to talk on stage. That was not one of my strong points and the devil taunted me with: "How are you ever going to get up there and tell them about Jesus; you don't talk. You'll never be successful at it." I was extremely stressed and troubled over it all.

It was a dreary, rainy morning and in spite of feeling quite depressed, I went to the meeting anyway.

I arrived a wee bit late, and the music was already underway. In between songs, people gave their testimonies and the service seemed to go on for a long time. All through the worship, I felt God speaking to me in my spirit, saying, "I want you to ask them to pray for you, Terri."

I said, "God, I can't do that. I can't share all of my private business with everyone."

God didn't give up though. He continued to woo me, and lead me, and draw me. He put the question to me again and again, but still, I did not respond.

Milton Carroll, who was leading the prayer, was about to close out when he finally said, "God just showed me that Terri needs us to pray for her." He was absolutely right.

GOD MET ME IN MY TRIAL

Nobody knew how much I was struggling in that moment but I didn't want anyone to know. In fact, growing up I was never one to show emotion around others. At that point I was overwhelmed by how much the Lord loved me. He reached down to do for me what I could not do for myself; it was beyond miraculous. I began to weep uncontrollably in front of everyone but that no longer mattered. It was as if He and I were the only ones in the room.

They gathered around, laid hands on me, and prayed. Then a lady who was standing near me said, "I see a wall in front of you. It's so high you can't get over it. It's so long you can't get around it. God said to tell you He is going to walk you right through it."

Just like the old Dottie Rambo song says, "He looked beyond my fault and saw my need." Even though I was saved in 1980, the Lord began a new work in me that day. I have never been the same since.

WHEN SALVATION CAME

You see I was already saved; that is, I had already accepted Jesus Christ as my Savior. I had made that decision among friends several years before. Let me tell you about that.

I'm sure God knocked on the door of my heart many times over the years, but I was just too busy to hear Him. But God reached out to me through a friend of mine from years ago. Before he became a Christian, he would come listen to me sing in the Augusta area. Then at one point, he met a girl over in Charleston and he later married her.

Sometime after that, they accepted Jesus together and were telling everybody about it, asking other people if they were saved and if they'd like to accept Jesus too. I was about twenty-five at the time. Sometimes I'd visit them and even stay with them. They were both precious to me.

In the year 1980, on June 29th, I lost my Grandmother. I was devastated. These same friends were there to help me through my grief. They also invited me to attend their church. I experienced a kind of fellowship there that should exist in all churches.

While there, I talked with them about my grandmother's passing. I was asked, "Do you have the assurance that you're going to see her again?"

My answer was that I didn't know.

I knew in my heart that I "believed" because I grew up in church and received all those things, I heard preached, yet I hadn't personally accepted Jesus as my Savior. My family was very prominent in the church and I didn't want to embarrass them by coming forward. So, I didn't have that daily relationship with the Lord or have that special sense of assurance that only He can give.

My friends led me to accept Christ and it's a day I'll remember forever. I finally knew that my name was in the Lamb's Book of Life and that I would go to heaven and be able to see Grandmother again one day.

HE NEVER LEAVES US; HE NEVER FORGETS

Since that day I've found God's strength to endure life's difficulties because He's put a little bit of heaven inside of me.

The Bible says, ***"I can do all things through Christ which strengtheneth me,"*** (Philippians 4:13; KJV). He has proven those words to me over and over again for He has said, ***"I will never leave you nor forsake you,"*** (Hebrews 13:5; NKJV), and He hasn't.

God did not leave me. He did not forsake me. He did not forget me. And yet I felt a waning in my soul. That's because it wasn't God who had moved, it was me. He was and always is just as close as the mention of His name. And He was trying to tell me that He missed me, and He still had plans for my life.

When I first became a born-again believer, death was defeated and life had won. In other words, my life *would* have ended in eternal death. Instead, God gave me the gift of eternal life. But there was so much more.

MORE OF JESUS

Here's the thing: although I had accepted God's forgiveness years ago, I knew something was still missing. At that moment in that store room, I knew what it was. I had drifted away from God, and, I had lost that special fellowship with other Christian believers.

So, the Holy Spirit came upon me and filled my heart completely. God wrapped me up in His gentle love. I had never felt His presence in such a great way before. His Spirit overwhelmed me and I knew that I would never lose it. He was mine and I was His, forever.

One day it's going to be me doing the knocking. I'm going to knock on Heaven's door and He will say, "Welcome home Terri, my faithful daughter. I have prepared a place for you." Then I'll see my loved ones and friends; those who have accepted Him like I have. There will be no more night, no more blindness, no more darkness, no more sin; just love and fellowship with Jesus.

TODAY HE IS SEEKING YOU

Let me encourage you. You can call on God anytime, anywhere and He will draw close to you. He will see to your needs because He loves you with an everlasting love that never weakens and never falters.

If you haven't had the experience of asking Jesus into your life, I wish you would. Living under the weight of sin's guilt is too hard to bear. Jesus will carry that burden for you if you'll let Him. He's already paid the price. Now it's up to you to ask Him to forgive all the wrongs you've ever done. Then He'll come into your heart forevermore and give you a kind of peace that the world could never give.

Listen. Somebody's knockin'. He is standing at the door of your heart wanting to come in. What will you do with Jesus?

CHAPTER SEVENTEEN
NEW HORIZONS

NOT A BLIND SINGER
Life continued for me as a singer. I was invited to go back to my home state of Florida. I found myself in Orlando, playing at the Cheyenne Saloon and Opera House on West Church Street. It wasn't a Christian music event. Back then I was still performing wherever I had the opportunity. But I felt God's leading and I knew He was taking me in a new direction.

For now, God was taking me back to the region where I was born. It was a place where the world had given up on me, but God hadn't. Instead of the weak child who was supposed to die, God intervened and I became the child that went home, happy and healthy. Blind yes, but alive and well against all odds.

Now He was working miracles again and soon, new doors would open. I wouldn't need to sing in worldly places anymore; He was calling me into a world where I belonged.

CHRISTIAN MUSIC
I toured for a few years as a Country music singer, but even then, I'd sing *Amazing Grace* at the end of my shows. I loved the song and knew what a wretch I was. In spite of that, He saved me and made me clean. In my heart, I wanted to tell people that they could have a changed life in Him too.

Sometimes, at the end of those Country shows in different cities, certain people would approach me and say, "The Lord wants you to sing for Him." How could each person be saying the same thing when they didn't even know each other? I was amazed. Actually, I had already decided to pursue Gospel music after having met with Word Music, but at the same time I was afraid to make the change.

Then there was a woman whose name I don't recall. She said the Lord wanted her to call me and tell me, "The Lord wants you to sing Christian music." She didn't know who to call or where to begin. She said, "Dear God, these people will think I'm crazy if I try to call." But the thought just wouldn't let go of her.

I'm a firm believer that if the Lord wants you to do something, He's going to keep bringing it back to you. Well, she didn't want to do it but she got the phone book out and just started calling people named "Gibbs." Finally, she reached my sister-in-law, my brother Don's wife, Vicki. She told her the story, and Vicki said, "Why don't you write her a letter?"

Days later, the letter reached me. I read it and it made an impact on my heart. I knew the message was right. I just didn't know how the timing of it would work. I did finally give it all to the Lord and He opened the way for me to sing only Christian music. Since then, I've never looked back.

THE FIRST THING I'LL SEE

One of the songs I performed for the Gaither tour was, *The First Thing I'll See.* Here are the lyrics:

I have never seen a flower or a tree
Or the sky alive so blue on a summer's afternoon
I've never seen a sunrise or ocean waves at midnight
But one day, I'll have my sight
In a place where there's no night

R. Douglas Veer/Terri Gibbs

And, the first thing I'll see will be Jesus
The first thing I see will be my Lord
Then He'll look at me, and then,
He'll say, "Well done my faithful friend."
The first thing I see will be Jesus

I can hardly wait to see those pearly gates,
And I know the streets of pure gold
Ah, they will be something to behold
All around the crystal sea, I'll sing praises to my King
As I stand before the throne
there I'll worship Him alone

And, the first thing I'll see will be Jesus
The first thing I see will be my Lord
Then he'll look at me, and then
He'll say, "Well done my faithful friend."
The first thing I see will be Jesus

Yeah, He'll look at me and then
He'll say, "Well done my faithful friend."
The first thing I see will be Jesus

If you would like to download this song from YouTube, here is the link:
www.youtube.com/results?search_query=terri+gibbs

WHEN ONE DOOR CLOSES, ANOTHER DOOR OPENS

The time had come. In 1987, I decided to leave Country music and sing only for Christ. Since then, I've sung mostly in churches performing Christian concerts. I have tried to use those opportunities to tell people what the Lord has done for me. And I've shared that

85

they, too, can have the same Jesus in their lives; the one who came to me in that little back room in Nashville.

I went on to sign a contract with *Word Music*, a Christian company. Since that day I have never looked back. I changed from straight Country to Gospel music. But I soon found that people weren't as anxious to buy my albums. So of course, my income went way down. Even so, I was not going to compromise. I was going to sing what magnified the Lord, not what magnified the world.

I buckled down and started concentrating on my Christian roots. I wanted my music to count for God, and I knew I was on the right track because I had great inner peace about it.

My decision came with a price, however. That same year I had to put my big house up for sale. I had been there six years, but it was time to move on. I had an appointment to meet with a man on May 1, 1987. He was interested in buying my house. So, I flew from Nashville back to Grovetown for the meeting. The first day of May is known as May Day, also called flower day. Some folks give flower gifts on that day. Well God gave me two gifts that day.

First, the man liked my house so much he bought it. Secondly, that same day I met my-husband-to-be, David Daughtry. I'll share that part of the story with you in a little while.

ABOUT MY DAD

During the time I lived on Chamblin Road, my folks lived with me. But as time went along, Daddy became ill. He actually started getting sick in about 1983. He was diagnosed with some kind of irreparable heart condition. Back then they couldn't help him although today, they probably could have.

Daddy had to retire early from his job because his prognosis was not good. They gave him roughly two years to live. Finally, he passed away in his sleep at home, March 6, 1985, from a massive coronary. Momma stayed with me until I later sold the house in 1987.

MY HOME IN HEAVEN

Selling my Chamblin Road house was a hard decision because it was very special. I know that in the world there are nicer homes than the one I had, but this house meant so much because I had never had anything of that caliber before.

The house has changed hands and has been renovated many times since then. It doesn't even resemble my original home, but it will always be in my memory no matter how much it's been altered. I often hear about it and ride by just for old time sake.

It wouldn't surprise me if my home in Heaven will be something like that one. I believe that's just the way Jesus is. The Lord knows the number of hairs on our head so I am sure He knows better than anyone those things we hold dear.

After Daddy died, Momma and I both needed the Lord's strength. In the midst of my sorrow, the big house and the success offered very little in the way of comfort. But the Lord was a safe refuge for me.

The Bible says, ***"The LORD is like a strong tower, where the righteous can go and be safe,"*** (Proverbs 18:10; GNT).

The Lord was my rock and my strong tower. He alone was the one I could truly lean on. What could ease the pain of losing my father? I found a certain joy that only Jesus could give. He filled the empty places.

You may think it's strange to talk about having joy in times of sadness, but it is possible. Daddy was in Heaven because he had accepted Christ. Knowing I would see him one day brought much joy to my heart. Yes, our family lost our *earthly* father but our heavenly Father brought us through it.

CHAPTER EIGHTEEN
FOR BETTER OR FOR WORSE

A GREAT EMPTINESS

Leaving Chamblin Road was a step in the right direction. I was on my way to getting my life back in tune with God. Even though I loved Country music and all the people in it, I felt that God was calling me to a different life, so leaving it was right for me.

At the same time, I was experiencing a new kind of emptiness. Every time an appearance was over and the applause died down, I found myself feeling lonely. I wasn't as fulfilled as I thought I would be. There was something incomplete in my life but I just didn't have the answers.

There's a Scripture that says, ***"For what is a man profited, if he shall gain the whole world and lose his own soul? Or what shall a man give in exchange for his soul?"*** (Matthew 16:26; KJV).

Well, I hadn't lost my soul or anything like that, but having the whole world before me had blurred my sense of God's will for me. On the outside, everything was exciting, but on the inside, I wondered how God was going to fix things.

We often don't realize how much God loves us. Why? Because we don't love ourselves half the time so how could we even begin to imagine His love for us, especially the way we are.

Some people think, "God is mad at me for my mistakes." But He's not. He will always forgive us if we ask Him.

When God showed me how much Jesus loves me, I also knew He was concerned about the loneliness I felt.

MONOPOLY NIGHT

I was still spending much time in Nashville when my house went up for sale. As I mentioned, I had to fly back to Grovetown one particular day to show the house. Now I hadn't met David yet, (my soon to be husband). He was living in Toccoa, Georgia, at the time and worked for an insurance company. But David had family in Grovetown and had gone to visit them around that same time.

It so happened that David got sick during his visit and had to go to the hospital. The doctors found that he had severe appendicitis and needed surgery right away. So that kept him in Grovetown longer than planned, and it all worked out in my favor. Well, I don't mean it was good about him having appendicitis! But his illness sort of put us together at just the right time so we could meet.

It's a long story but David had a sister, Teresa. She had written a song for her daddy but she didn't know how to write the music for it. A mutual friend knew me and suggested Teresa call me for some help, so she did. A short time later she said, "Hey Terri, won't you come over and play monopoly with us tonight?" And that's how I met David.

Well, Monopoly happened to be my favorite board game. By memory, I learned all the names of the board stops, like Park Place, the Boardwalk, the Railroads, and the "Go to Jail" corner. I also figured out how to read the dice by the indented dots on the top so I'd know how many places I could move. I actually got pretty good at it.

David and his family loved to play Monopoly but they hadn't played for quite some time because David always won. The night I was invited over, David won again. He boasted to his sister about how good of a player he was. She told me what he said and I fired back, "Well you tell him I'll come back tomorrow and play him one-on-one. I'll show him I can beat him!"

The challenge was on. The next night we met again at Teresa's house and just the two of us played. Sure enough, I beat him! Later, I wondered if perhaps he let me win just so he could be nice to me and get my attention. I don't know. But it sure broke the ice for us that first day of May in 1987; the day that's called "May Day" or "Flower Day".

WE SAID "I DO"

David and I spent time getting to know each other after that. About four months had gone by when he invited me to come over to his house for supper. I accepted.

He cooked me up a fancy steak that night and "umm umm", boy, it was good! I sort of thought something was in the wind because of the nice dinner and all. We were sitting there watching Jeopardy on television when suddenly David, like a gentleman, got down on one knee and asked me if I would marry him. It was a very special moment in my life. Of course, I said yes.

We were engaged when I was thirty-three and David was thirty-five. The date was September 12, 1987. I was actually still touring at the time and I had just started recording with New Cannan Records. We remained engaged for several months and on April 28, 1988, we were married at Dearing Full Gospel Church.

We lived in Augusta for about a year but felt I needed to be closer to Nashville so I could have better access to the Christian music scene. We eventually moved to Nashville in May of 1989. God was blessing us in many ways.

DAVID NUMBER TWO

Before long there was a new thrill in my life. We found out we were expecting a child. Our son David Daughtry II, was born October 20, 1989, in Nashville, Tennessee. He was such a wonderful blessing.

I didn't want to take too much time off, so at my very next engagement, I brought little David on stage with me for the first time. He was only four weeks old. Maybe that's where he got the bug to become a musician and Country singer.

During my Christian music concerts that followed, I would hold David in my lap and sing and the people loved it. Through the years I often had him come up with me for a few moments. Eventually, he would sing a song or two with me as well.

I don't think David has ever been nervous about being on stage; he didn't know you were supposed to be. Music was ingrained in him. I think he heard music from the womb; that's how he came to love it as much as I do.

When I did do a concert, folks would sometimes say, "I wish David would sing more," or "I wish you'd go back to Country music." If they only realized how hard that lifestyle was on our family. They meant well, I know. I love my fans and appreciate them. But I felt I had to start drawing the line.

CHANGES WERE COMING

So, while in Nashville I continued my busy touring schedule, but I knew it would have to slow down because our son, David, was growing older. He had to have a more stable environment, especially since he would soon be starting school. We also felt it was important for him and for my husband and I to be near our kin folk.

Our child had to be our first priority, not Nashville. While I loved performing music, it was time to put it on hold. It was time for my domestic life to take center stage, not my career.

So, changes were coming. A lifestyle of traveling, interviews, and concert appearances wouldn't be easy for a family. I would have to back out of the entertainment world. A serious decision had to be made.

We decided to leave Nashville in August of 1990 and we moved home to Georgia. I've never looked back or had any regret. It was family first, all the way.

CHAPTER NINETEEN
FAMILY LIFE

A SWEET CHILD
Raising David was a joy. When he finally started school, I wanted so much for him to like it. I looked forward to attending the Mother's Day programs, the outings, and other things. I didn't want to let myself get too busy and miss out.

My son would come home from school all excited and tell me about everything going on. I was glad he liked school and did so well. It helped that he was so outgoing too. But I wanted to dig a little deeper and know more about *what* he liked. One day I asked him, "David, do you like school?"

He answered, "Oh yes ma'am."

I continued, "Well, tell me, what's your favorite part of the day?" I figured he'd say recess or lunch or something. He surprised me when he said, "My favorite part is when I come home in the afternoon and you're there, Mom." That was God's way of telling me that I was right where I needed to be. I didn't need to fill my life with traveling.

Young David loved people and it showed. For example, whenever we did travel and were at a hotel, we would often go to the snack machines at the end of the hall. If there was a bellman around my son would say, "Hi, I'm David Daughtry." Then I'd laugh and think, "That man doesn't care what your name is." He was that way at school too. He didn't have a problem getting along with others.

David was very caring too. Once, when he was about ten or eleven, we had gone out to the grocery store. Somehow, I missed my step, tumbled off of the curb and scraped my knee. This child of mine took me home right away, made me sit down, cleaned the wound really well, put disinfectant on it and a band-aid. I felt totally taken care of. What a sweet child.

MY BEST FRIEND

I spent a lot of time with my son in his growing up years. People say you shouldn't be friends with your kids; you should just be a parent. But David and I were very close. We enjoyed doing things together, like reading before bed time. I'd have my braille copy and he'd have a print copy so he could look at the pictures.

There was one particular evening when he was getting ready for bed. He said, "Momma would you scratch my back?" I said "Sure . . . would you scratch mine too?" He said, "O.K."

So, I took my time, I did my very best; I did a really good job. And when I got all finished, I sat and waited. Then I waited some more, but still nothing happened. Finally, I said, "David. Are you gonna scratch my back?" And he laughed and said, "Oh Momma. I was just kiddin'." What a child he was!

David has always been my best friend. You see, soon after I was married, God spoke to me one day with that unmistakable soft, still voice. He promised me that He would send a child to be with me in my later years. Yes, God's promises are true because David has been a great blessing. He's helped me work out many, many issues and he gives me sound advice. He's very intelligent.

CHURCH CONCERTS

People have wondered how active I remained in music after we started our family. While my son was young, I still traveled to various churches. I just didn't do it to the degree I had before. I made it more of a local thing rather than a long-distance thing. I would travel maybe two or three hours at the most for an engagement and once in a while, if a church budget could afford it, they would provide my airline tickets and funds for an assistant so I could travel further. But it didn't happen too often. My main focus was being a stay at home mom.

I also had what you might call an unusual gig. A few times a month I sang and played piano at Augusta's Borders Book Store. You may think it strange to sing at a bookstore but there was a section inside of the store with tables and chairs. Folks could sit there and read and drink coffee or soft drinks. It was nice that I could play in a place where no alcohol was served. And, they let me sing Christian songs in addition to nice, pleasant, love songs that were enjoyable for all.

AND THE BEAT GOES ON

In 1994 I was extremely blessed to meet and sing with the Bill Gaither group during a Homecoming Tour. As I became more well-known people would refer to me as "Terri Gibbs the blind singer." My response to that was, "It's not that I'm a blind singer. I'm a singer that happens to be blind."

God definitely worked things out years ago. I can never thank Him enough for all He's done for me. That's why I perform Christian Concerts. It's my way of glorifying God, and it serves as a platform to share my faith with others.

I used to sing in nightclubs and the like. In that world, everyone is always thinking about how to get ahead, get more money, and buy more things. My *thing* is to love God with all my heart and soul and strength. And now I have a wonderful husband and son to share my love with, too. God has fulfilled all of my dreams and I can even say, I'm not lonely anymore.

Below is a snapshot of our home-life. It's from a particular Christmas when my husband, David, wrote an article for the newspaper about what the holidays meant to him.

"A SPECIAL CHRISTMAS,"

[Hi. This is David Daughtry Senior.] Christmas has always been a special time of year for me and all of my family. A Christmas that brings back some fond memories is the Christmas of 1995. My son "little" David the second was six at the time and like most children his age, he was excited about all the gifts. We would take turns so each could see what everyone was getting. When his turn came to open his gifts, he was just bubbling over.

He opened the first gift and loudly exclaimed, "Oh boy. Socks. I got new socks!" Then it was on to the next one. "Wow. Underwear. I got new underwear!" And that's the way it went.

You see my mom always wanted to make sure that we all had new, clean underwear in case we were ever in an accident.

Later in February, my mom got to leave this earth to spend eternity with the Greatest Gift ever given. That gift was from the Heavenly Father who sent His Son. He did it so we could spend eternity with Him in heaven.

It's my prayer that all of you who read this will open that Gift; the gift of Jesus Christ. And if you do, I can almost guarantee you that when you reach heaven and celebrate your first Christmas, my mom will give you new underwear and socks!

From my family: we wish you all a very MERRY CHRISTMAS!

--David W. Daughtry Senior

CHAPTER TWENTY
THE END OF AN ERA

A WORRISOME SITUATION
I was enjoying family life with my husband and son but the years passed quickly. Then sadness touched our lives. My husband began having health problems and went into the hospital in May of 2007, because of pain and neuropathy in his legs caused by diabetes. He was released that same month and struggled at home until December.

In early December, David started having trouble breathing. He was getting along so badly that family members strongly encouraged him to go to the emergency room. He agreed and the doctors wanted to admit him. They told him if he went home, he could possibly die.

We tried hard to talk him into staying because we were so afraid for him. None-the-less, he insisted on going home in spite of the doctor's advice. He said to me later that night, "I'm sorry I couldn't stay at the hospital like you wanted me to." He went on to explain that he needed to take care of some important business.

As I shared with you previously, Christmas was David's favorite time of year. He loved to go shopping for family gifts and he and young David would usually go Christmas shopping together. Sometimes I would go too, and they would buy gifts for me right under my nose. But of course, I wouldn't have a clue about what they purchased.

They were always thinking about each family member's heart's desires, so if there was ever something special one of us wanted, that was the time it was bought. My husband, David, wanted to make sure all of us had what we needed. Because of David's concern over the coming holiday season, he asked his daughter, Bobbie Jo, to take over the check book and said, "Here are the lists. Will you promise me to make sure that Christmas is taken care of?"

ADMITTED AGAIN

The next morning, he was quite confused and incoherent and his legs had begun to weep. His condition had become very serious. I knew he had to go back to the hospital. I couldn't leave it up to him anymore; I had to intervene. I called an ambulance and then said to him, "You have got to go back to the hospital; you are not doing well; you don't have a choice."

Doctors once again made a diagnoses: David had sepsis, an infection in the bloodstream. He kept asking them to let him sit up a little bit or at least raise the head of his bed because he was having extreme difficulty breathing. But he was hooked up to so many machines, it wasn't really possible to alter his position.

We stayed with him all of that day. After that, the nurse said, "You need to let us do our job here." Then he said to me, "I just want you to know how much I love you . . . I'm going to die." And I said, "No you're not because I'm praying for you."

DEATH SPEAKS

Young David so much wanted his daddy to come home that he went home to straighten everything up. He wanted things to be perfect for him. That night I turned in around midnight and David stayed up to finish things around the house.

He was very tired but he was hungry. So, he fixed himself some macaroni and cheese and sat down in his dad's chair to eat it. When he was done, he placed the bowl on the table beside the chair and fell asleep.

He told me later that he had a dream and heard his dad talking to him. His dad said, "Now David, get that bowl and put it in the dishwasher. Don't leave it on the table. I just wanted to tell you I love you. Take care of your momma."

All of a sudden, the phone rang. It was the hospital saying that my husband's heart had stopped and we needed to come to the hospital right away. The doctors had to shock him several times to start his heartbeat again. Then they placed him in a drug induced coma hoping things would improve.

We found out later that he had had pneumonia so the CPR they performed on him was not effective. As a result, he was without oxygen for thirteen minutes. Then, several days later when they tried to wake him up, he was unresponsive. The cortex of his brain had been damaged and the longer it took for him to awaken, the less likely it would be that he would. The prognosis was not good, so on December 31st, they moved him to a "specialty hospital" to see if they could do something more for him there.

At that point, much prayer had gone up for David and I had a lot of faith that he would be healed. But things did not improve. By the middle of February, the doctors told us that the life support machines were keeping him alive but his death was imminent. An important decision had to be made.

I was perplexed and said to my son, "I prayed so hard for God to heal him." And he gently replied, "Momma, God did heal him. He just healed him in heaven." God doesn't always answer prayer the way we think, but God does answer according to His perfect will.

I had been married to my husband almost 20 years. Now I was faced with a very hard decision but I made that decision because I knew it was for the best. I did everything I knew to do to help Him get well. On February 18, I gave permission to allow the hospital to turn off his life-support system. That, of course, ended his life. He passed away February 19th, 2008.

I also believe God took David's soul before his body expired. I believe that when my husband came to young David in that dream the night of December 9th, that's when he went to heaven.

CHAPTER TWENTY-ONE
BEAUTY FOR ASHES

FORLORN BUT NOT FORSAKEN

My son, David, was only eighteen years old when his daddy passed away. It happened just a few weeks before he graduated from high school in May. I felt like my whole world was going to cave in right then but I couldn't give in to that. God had blessed me to be a mother and with that came responsibilities that I had to live up to.

Besides dealing with my own grief I needed to see young David through his ups and downs. I had to be there for my son. Whether he was eight years old or eighteen, he needed me.

Suddenly, I was not only a single Mom, but a single Mom without sight. On top of that, my son, David, was a teen-aged boy who was ready to go out into the world. I needed the Lord to help me guide and direct him so that he could make sound decisions.

The next year or so was going to be a challenge but I knew God would be merciful to me. I knew He'd hold me up. David may have lost his daddy, but I had a Daddy to call on for both of us. He is a Daddy who has promised He would ***"never leave us nor forsake us,"*** (See Hebrews 13:5). He promised in His Word that He would be ***"a father to the fatherless and a husband to the widows,"*** (See Psalm 68:5).

So, I called on God for strength to help me with the many situations ahead. I knew I didn't have that kind of strength but I knew God did, and He was going to take care of us! I can truly say God came through. He was there for me in every way and gave me the kind of peace that passes all understanding.

FROM ME TO YOU

Are you facing loss in your life right now? Whoever you might be reading this, I'd like to offer comfort in your trial. Maybe you don't know which way to turn. I'd like to help point the way. I know Someone who will give you His shoulder to cry on. He understands. And He will lift you up and set your feet on a straight path.

You might be blinded by sorrow and wondering how you'll live through it. You may be wondering if God even cares. Maybe you're blaming Him. Maybe you're asking, "Why me God? Why did you let this happen?" Maybe you're thinking you're in this and you're all alone. Someone keeps rocking the boat and keeping you off balance. It's not a pleasant place to be.

I know those feelings of helplessness. But I have found strength in the Lord. Please know that you can too.

I want to share some verses from the third chapter of Psalms, (NKJV). In it, you'll find God's assurance. He knows your needs; He's listening. David said it this way:

> *4 I cried to the Lord with my voice,*
> *And He heard me from His holy hill. Selah*
> *5 I lay down and slept;*
> *I awoke, for the Lord sustained me.*
> *8 Salvation belongs to the Lord.*
> *Your blessing is upon Your people. Selah*

You can lean on God; He will never let you down. I've had to wait for Him to do things in His time, but without a doubt, I can say He is the one who saw me through. I know He will help you too. I hope you'll meditate on these words. His words are so much more important than anything I have written here.

CHAPTER TWENTY-TWO
FOND MEMORIES

FUNNY STUFF

I continued raising my son alone. While going forward I found myself looking back to when he was a little boy. I remembered so many things.

For example, when David wanted to show me something, he would come and get me by the hand and place my fingers on the object. He understood I couldn't see so he would help me touch it. In the same way, God was putting His hand on me, that I might understand things better and have the same confidence to go on.

I also remembered how I used to keep David in certain areas of the house where I knew he was safe. But I couldn't do that now. He was nearly a grown young man. All I could do is pray and ask God to direct him.

And I remember some funny stuff that happened, too. When David was very young, he would sometimes be so quiet I wouldn't hear him or suspect what he might be up to.

One night his daddy came home from work and said, "Terri! Why is there salt and pepper all over the floors?" Of course, it was because I couldn't hear my precious son emptying the salt and pepper shakers throughout the entire house. It was everywhere, in every room. It was fun for him, but not for his daddy and me. We had a good laugh about it later though.

Another situation that I had to deal with was during morning times. David liked to eat breakfast while watching TV. The thing was that he needed enough time to get dressed and ready for school. But the TV took all of his attention and sometimes he would almost miss the bus.

So, I had to set a new rule. I told him he couldn't watch TV in the mornings anymore because it distracted him too much and he didn't want to miss his ride. He seemed to comply so I thought I had solved the problem. The house was quiet while he ate his breakfast and everything seemed to be right on track. Good for me! Or so I thought.

One evening my husband came home and said, "Terri, why is the TV playing with the sound muted?" Well, I guess my son tricked me. He found out he could still watch TV even without the sound and I wasn't the wiser! It made for another good laugh.

OUT FOR A WALK

Grovetown was still a pretty small town when David was young. I remember when McDonalds opened in our area. We thought we had died and gone to heaven. Now David had become my eyes even from a young age. So, one hot summer day, we decided to go for a walk just like we always did and decided to go to McDonalds for lunch.

After starting out, it felt like we had walked for quite a while. It was getting hot and I was ready for some food and refreshment. Like a child would ask a parent I said, "David. Are we almost there?"

He said, "Yes, Momma. I can see it."

So, I was encouraged that we'd be there soon. And we walked some more, and we walked some more. By this time, I felt like I was ready to have a heat stroke. I said, "David. I thought you said we were almost there?"

"We are momma. I can see it from here!" I guess I didn't realize how far a sighted person could see, and I certainly didn't realize how far McDonalds was either.

ADVICE FOR PARENTS

We had our fun back then when my husband was still alive. He and I worked out everything together. Now things were going to be different. Now there was no husband to help me. Now all I had was his picture hanging over my fireplace and his neatly folded military flag from the funeral boxed and placed on top of my piano. I surely have missed him.

So, I prayed that God would help me be a single parent. I said, "Lord, now that my son is older please make it even easier than when he was a child and when I had a husband here to help me."

Someone asked me once, "Is there anything you would share to help Mothers who have a blind child to raise?"

I didn't know why I was asked this question. I didn't raise a blind child. *I* was the blind child growing up. But I think the experience of being a parent is universal whether one's child is blind or not. So, I told the person, "My advice would be to work at having a wonderful relationship with your child. Be best friends.

"Furthermore, be the best example you can be so your child will grow up to be the best adult he or she can be. Tell him, 'You have to believe you can succeed, because you can. Never doubt it.'

"Most importantly, teach your child about love and kindness. It will change their world and it will change the way they live life."

CHAPTER TWENTY-THREE
FROM A BROTHER'S POINT OF VIEW – PART I

MEMORIES OF MY YOUTH

I have two brothers and no sisters. I could have been a spoiled brat, or one who was always picked on, or one who was treated like a princess. I was none of the above. I was treated like a regular kid without much thought about my blindness. That was great for me. My brothers tell the story this way . . .

MY BROTHER DON

Hi, I'm Don, and I was named after Daddy. Daddy was sort of a prideful man; a one-word man. He would only have to tell you something one time and you'd know that he meant it. At the same time, I remember how he would give you his last dollar out of his pocket. If we were needing something, he knew we really wanted He would say, "Alright, you deserve it."

Daddy went out of his way to raise us up not to lie, not tell stories, and to tell the truth no matter how bad it hurt. He had a lot of qualities that people don't have today. You never had to question where he was coming from. He always carried a good reputation. He was honest but he didn't take any sass from anyone.

I don't know why Daddy never sang much although he did sing in church with his two brothers. He really could sing well and had a good voice. Terri has a lot of those same talents which I guess she got from him. Even today, when I meet people who hear my name, *Gibbs,* they say, "Hey you ain't kin to that singer Terri Gibbs are you?" And I'm always glad to say "Yeah. I sure am."

As for Terri, we didn't ever see her as being handicapped. The truth is, it was more like we were the ones with a disability. Even as children, Terri always seemed to be way ahead of us. She couldn't see, but her other senses were very strong and finely tuned.

HIDE-AND-SEEK

I remember one time we were all stuck in the house and we decided to play hide-and-seek. We were thinking that because she couldn't see it would make the game pretty easy for us!

When it was our turn to go hide, I went into the dining room and got in the corner and was real quiet. In a few minutes, she came down the hallway to the doorway of the room. She just stopped and stood there a minute.

I had learned that when Terri took her hand and placed it on her cheek, she was concentrating real hard. So, I stood there in the corner watching her. After about forty-five seconds or so, she started grinning. She felt her way across the room. Then she stopped and listened a bit, and then moved along some more. She slowly worked her way over to the corner. Finally, she reached out and touched me.

For the longest time, I was mystified over how she found me. I guess I wasn't old enough to figure it out. But when we got older, she told me what she was doing in those moments. She was actually listening. Listening to what? She said she could hear me breathing! That was just one of the many things she developed that was special.

SPINNING RECORDS

Another thing about Terri is that she has always been extremely independent. That was true from the time she was a child and on up into her adult years. Growing up, Mom and Dad had a home over on Belair Road. But they also bought a mobile home that they put out there on the property. Terri was excited to live there on her own so she could listen to her music.

She had a huge collection of 45 rpm records, which I imagine she still has. I can remember, I'd often go over there and she'd be playing her records just as loud as can be. She'd listen to many different types of music and I would be so amazed that once she heard a song, she could remember it. And she could turn around and play it and sing it right back.

Terri also has a love for animals. She always had a cat around even though she was allergic to them. She loved dogs too and would take them in and talk to them and treat them as if they were a person. They'd respond to her in turn, in the same sweet way.

THE BIG TIMES

When Terri got her first Country Music award and was becoming famous in the music world, us boys were about twelve and eighteen and nobody knew us anymore as Don and Dale. They would see us and say, "Hey, you're Terri's brother." But that didn't bother us. We never took it personally because of course, we were proud of her.

A lot of times, Terri was called to go out on the road. The bus would come to the house and pick her up. And sometimes if it was just a short trip for a few days or overnight, she would take me with her.

One time we were going down to Jacksonville, Florida so she could open a show for Hank Williams

Junior. I got to see his big bus and meet many people I would never have met otherwise. I've met folks like the group *Alabama,* as she was in a concert with them. And I've met Jim Ed Brown and Jerry Clower and Dolly Parton. When I met Dolly Parton, she hugged my neck! I mean just think about that as a teenage boy to have Dolly Parton hug your neck! No, I've never forgotten that.

DOWN HOME COUNTRY FOLKS

Well, Terri had a modest upbringing. We never were fancy folks. We were just country people. Terri and the rest of us grew up on a small dairy farm. In 1962, Interstate Twenty came through and cut my grandfather's property in half. They kept a few cows after that but in time sold them and did a little bit of grow-crop farming. Then we just sort of *maintained* and barely lived.

When Terri became famous, we discovered we had relatives that just *came out of the woodwork.* In fact, people were suddenly coming out of nowhere, wanting to be part of the scene. They wanted to be attached to a famous person in some way.

There were a lot of interesting happenings that resulted from Terri's fame. I remember People Magazine came to the house one time and did an article on Terri. We had our pictures in the magazine too.

When Terri bought that big house on Chamblin Road in Grovetown, we ended up all going to live with her. Then in March 1985, Daddy died there. Those years were very special and I'll always remember them in my heart.

CHAPTER TWENTY-FOUR
FROM A BROTHER'S POINT OF VIEW – PART II

MY BROTHER DALE

Hi, I'm Dale. I'm twelve years younger than Terri so she and I were pretty much on opposite ends of the spectrum as far as siblings go. There's much I missed during the years she was growing up but we always had a terrific relationship.

We grew up on Granddaddy's dairy farm. Don was older than me and he was all about tractors and cows and all that farm stuff. But we liked to play together and I do remember playing hide-and-seek with Terri. And do you know that she'd catch us every time?!

FUN AT PLAY

Speaking of hide-and-seek, I have my own slant on how we would play the game. One night, Momma and Daddy were gone and we wanted to play so Terri suggested that to make it fair, we should turn out all the lights. As a matter of fact, she wanted us to turn off the main breaker so she would be sure we were in the dark.

Don and I went and hid and Terri was supposed to find us. I thought about hiding in a lot of different places but I realized she'd probably find me. I needed a good hiding place so I decided to go into Momma's bedroom and hide in the closet.

I got in there and shuffled the clothes around until I could get behind them. Then I pulled them all back in place over me. I was so sure she wouldn't find me this time.

Before too long, I heard her find Don so I knew she'd be looking for me next. I could hear her walking in the other rooms and down the hallway. Then she came into Momma and Daddy's bedroom and stood for a minute. A few seconds later she came to the closet.

I could just barely make out her shape in the dark of the room as she stood there. Then she said, "Dale, you may as well come out, I know you're in there." I didn't say anything.

She spoke again, "Dale, I know you're in there so come on out." I still didn't move a muscle. I thought for sure I had her. It was beginning to get hot in there but I held my breath and stayed perfectly still. I just knew I had her fooled. Then she began to pull at the clothes until she touched me. I was caught.

WHAT'S HER SECRET?

I said, "Terri, how did you know? I didn't move a hair and I didn't make a noise. I even held my breath once you were in the room. How did you figure it out?" She put her hand to her ear and said, "I didn't hear you, I smelled you and I could feel the heat from the closet."

I said, "What? You *smelled* me? That can't be right. I don't need a bath and there's nothing on me that smells. How did you know?"

She said, "I'm not talking about perfume and stuff like that. What I'm saying is that you all have your own smell. Don smells one way, Momma another way, Daddy another way, and you have your own smell too. I smelled you."

You know when you're eleven years old and no bigger around than a stick you can get into places and practically fold yourself up to hide so I thought she would really have to search out that house to find me.

But now I'm six feet two, and two hundred fifty-five pounds and there's no easy way to get myself into tight places anymore.

OTHER FUN STUFF

Terri also liked to play Yahtzee and Monopoly. As for Monopoly, she had memorized the entire game board. As a youngster, I'd get frustrated because she would keep winning. So, when I'd wrongly count the spaces on purpose and put her on Boardwalk or something to put her at a disadvantage, she'd catch me; she already had the spaces counted out in her mind.

She would say, "No wait a minute, that's not right. That has to go over one place because there's a railroad in between there." She'd tell me where her marker was supposed to be and I'd have to agree, "Yeah you're right." And I'd have to put the little horse or whatever on the right square. She was amazing.

DAVID JOINS THE FAMILY

I remember when Terri met her husband David. Don and I weren't sure why he was interested in her since she was blind. We didn't want their relationship to be a big burden on him. We were younger but we were protective of Terri.

As the relationship developed, I had a gut feeling that David knew it would cost him his life if he ever did Terri any harm. That's the way we boys were about our sister and that's the way we'll always be.

Another thing about Terri is that she loved to fish. Later, it became one of the nice things Terri and David could share with each other.

Anyway, we had about a two-acre pond on the farm that was stocked with Bass, Bluegill, and Catfish. Terri loved to get out there and catch 'em; she never tired of it. She would sit on a bucket and fish just as long as you would want to stay out there with her. She'd say, "Okay I got one". She'd reel it in, take it off the hook, bait the hook back up, and try again.

So, when Terri and David were married, they used to go up to the mountains, to the Tennessee River and fish the trout streams. David would put a lure on the line and she would do the rest. Terri surprised them all when she caught a rainbow trout that was six pounds or better. We heard later that it was the largest trout ever taken out of that area. I think she kept that one and had it mounted.

TERRI AND CRITTERS

I have to say, too, that Terri loved animals. I don't care if it was a cat, a dog, or a horse. She loved them all. She even had pet chickens. She would squat to the ground and the chickens would come to her to be petted. She loved that. She loved to pet all kinds of critters.

She also became fascinated with the old farm tractor. She loved getting up into it with Daddy to ride around the farm. She loved the farm, the animals and helping to raise the garden. She would always be in the middle of shelling peas, cracking pecans and all of those kinds of things. She's definitely a county lady at heart.

STEAK AND ALE

A memory that still hangs with me is when Terri would sing every night at the Steak and Ale in Augusta.

She was getting pretty well known and was making some nice money too. So, one night, she wanted to take Don and me out for a nice meal. We were just young, skinny boys and it was a treat to ever go out and eat anywhere. One thing for sure: we loved steak dinners.

To me, steak was like "the Holy Grail" of dining and Terri was going to feed us. Oh man, that was a big deal! And it was Prime Rib Night! I was as thin as a rail but they kept bringing me that prime rib. I ate five of them! Terri couldn't believe it. But she was thrilled to do that for me and my brother. I'll never forget it. She's always had such a giving heart.

When Terri became famous, I was so proud of her. She had a beautiful voice and a great talent, and everybody knew it. When I was younger, I thought, "It's a shame that she's blind. She has so much talent but she'll never be able to do anything with it."

Then her dreams came to pass and it was like, "Wow!" Then I realized the possibilities. I thought about people like Ronnie Milsap and Stevie Wonder and Ray Charles. Terri wasn't the first blind person to make it, and she won't be the last. Yes, I was very proud that she made it like she did. Since my teenage years until now, I have always been proud to have Terri as my sister, and I still am.

CHAPTER TWENTY-FIVE
PUTTING IT ALTOGETHER

TERRI'S BEEPER

In the writing of this book, I Doug Veer, did record several interviews over the telephone with Terri's family. Then I'd listen back and transcribe the audio.

Dale told me a story about a beeper Terri had. He explains, "Terri used to take me on the road with her sometimes. That's when she traveled in her bus. I remember one time we were out there somewhere and she told me she had forgotten her beeper. She needed it to retrieve messages from her answering machine by talking to her home phone remotely. She'd dial her home number and the beeper would send out a signal that activated her machine. It worked no matter where she was.

"But this particular day she had left the device at home. Frustrated over what to do, she decided to use her voice. Now you need to realize Terri has a wide vocal range and is also gifted with perfect pitch. Perfect pitch is the ability to hear a musical tone and identify the actual note.

"She knew the tone from the beeper was 'G', which was one and a half octaves above middle 'C'. She didn't have a piano nearby but knew the note she needed to voice. So, she dialed up her home number and when she heard the prompt, she hummed the sound that the beeper would have made into the phone. And voila! The machine--all the way over in Grovetown, Georgia--kicked in and reeled back her messages. Any questions?"

This author said, "What a hoot! We had some belly laughs over that whole story. Terri enjoyed it as much as I did because it brought back wonderful memories for her. How nice is that?

"Over and over, I can see Terri's heart, and I can see what a great person she is. She loved taking her younger brothers with her on road trips when she could. She never forgot the people she loved or left them out. Even though she was enveloped in fame, she was never taken by it. To me, that's a special lady. And she hasn't changed one bit. She's still the same person today."

CHAPTER TWENTY-SIX
MY FRIEND, COMPANION, AND GUIDE

MY FRIEND "BIRDIE"

One of my best friends was my guide dog, *Birdie*. I got him July 31st of 2002, long before my husband died. I had him a little more than ten years and I loved him very much. Our friendship was different from a human friendship, but even so, I became greatly attached to him as my friend, companion, and guide.

Today, I live without a guide dog. I haven't been able to forget Birdie; he's kind of irreplaceable. If I would get, say, another German Shepherd, I probably couldn't stand to reach down and touch his fur. It would remind me too much of my dear Birdie. I could get a Labrador; they're supposed to be great dogs for the blind too. But I guess I'm just not ready yet. So I'm learning to adapt without a guide dog; however, from time to time I do miss that special help.

One of the hardest things I've ever had to live through was losing Birdie. As age came upon him, he began to stumble. His hips and hind legs had become weak which hindered his walking. He was still doing his job for me but it was getting harder and harder all the time. It was sad for him I'm sure because I know he loved me and wanted to protect me.

I took him to the veterinarian but after he was examined and we got the test results back, the vet said he was suffering from crippling arthritis in his hips, and it was also affecting his heart. Because his heart was weak, he was losing strength and couldn't move very well anymore.

To make things worse, he was "my eyes", but he was also losing his sight. He had formed cataracts in both eyes and would have needed an operation to correct the problem. After that he would have needed eye drops several times a day which would have been a hardship for me. I was willing to retire him and keep him as a pet, but I didn't get the chance.

STORMS OF LIFE

Birdie's health started going down a couple of years after I had lost my husband. Emotions on top of emotions were piling up on me and I had to deal with them as best as I could. It felt like I was in a tiny rowboat in the middle of a storm at sea. One wave after another washed over me, taking away my sense of security and control.

First, my husband died. Then my dog became crippled. Then my son was accepted to a college in a town nearly four hours away. I was really glad for him but I missed him so. All of a sudden there was a lot going on in my life.

One Wednesday night, my friend, Kathy, and her husband and I were coming home from Augusta. I had left Birdie with David that day because his arthritis was affecting him. We were trying to get home before dark, hoping to make it to church on time. My son and his fiancée, Chelsey, had some time off from school (in South Georgia). David came to stay with me. His fiancée, Chelsey, had stopped by to pick him up, as they were obligated to be somewhere later on.

Birdie had been outside to do his business but when Chelsey called him, he couldn't get back up the porch steps. She called us to let us know what was happening and we all decided they should take Birdie to the vet. At that point the doctor gave him a shot to relieve the pressure on his spine. Then they scheduled a follow up appointment for Friday, hoping the shot would help his situation.

Upon returning, David and Chelsey decided to leave Birdie outside just in case he might have an accident in the house. I was on my way home anyway and knew I would be there soon.

WHERE'S MY BIRDIE

That Wednesday night we pulled into the driveway. I heard Birdie howling from the side yard. He wanted to come and greet me but he couldn't walk. The three of us hurried to his side but found he couldn't even get up. He could pull himself forward a little with his front legs but that's all. His hind legs were useless. I cried. After all the years he had helped me, I now was unable to help him.

I told Kathy to get me a pillow and some blankets. When she came back her husband, Doug, wanted to lift Birdie's head to put the pillow under it. That's when I told him, "No, the pillow is for me."

He asked, "What do you mean? What are you gonna do?"

I replied, "I'm going to sleep out here with Birdie until we can get him some help in the morning."

Doug said, "No Terri. You can't. It's way too cold out here . . . just hang on . . . we'll get him inside somehow."

Kathy and Doug had a plan. They got a large beach towel from the house and passed it under Birdie's belly just in front of his hind legs. Then Doug lifted Birdie's back end up off of the ground and walked him across the lawn, up the steps, and into the house on his front legs, like a wheel-barrow.

Birdie stayed in for the night but by the next morning he needed to go out again. He could get down the steps O.K. but he couldn't get back up. I was alone and couldn't help him with that, so I stayed outside with him until David came home. I went in the house periodically, but at one point when I did go back out, I couldn't find him.

I called him and thought I heard a whimper but when I walked toward him, he stopped. I called out to him again and he did the same thing. He whined a bit and stopped. That made it very difficult for me to figure out where he was.

I said, "Lord, this is not funny! Are you laughing at me? Show me where he is!" I guess I was very distraught. But as soon as I said that, Birdie cried for me and without a doubt, I knew it was the Lord showing me where he was and answering my prayer.

BYE BYE BIRDIE

Even though Birdie was suffering and I wanted him to be free of his pain, it was very hard for me to let him go. But I took him to his appointment the next day and was advised there wasn't much hope for my Birdie. The vet asked me if I'd be willing to let Birdie receive a shot to put him down. Giving Birdie that shot was like giving permission to kill my own child. It's one of the hardest decisions I've ever made.

In fact, it reminded me of when my husband was in the hospital and I had to agree to unplug the cords from his life-support system. In both cases, it was beyond difficult but I'm glad both of them are finally released from their pain.

Those final moments began on a Wednesday night in October. I had stayed home from church that evening to be with my dog. But two days later, on October 26, 2012, I had to have him put to sleep. It liked to have killed me.

Somebody once asked me, "What was it like for you to lose Birdie, your guide dog?"

I thoughtfully said, "Think of what it'd be like if you lost one of your kids. That's what it was like for me. It was like losing my child, my best friend and of course my companion all at the same time. He helped me do what I couldn't do on my own. He helped me to see where I was going and to know what was going on around me. Now he's not here for me and it has left a huge hole in my life; especially in my heart."

At the same time, I've often said, "I could have missed the pain, but then I would have missed the dance." That's the best way I can describe my loss. I hope I have helped you understand what losing Birdie was like.

CHAPTER TWENTY-SEVEN
MEMORIES TO WARM MY HEART

DOES HE BITE?

I have some great memories of Birdie to keep me going. Let me share some of them with you. For example, I would often go out with Birdie, and every once-in-a-while I'd run into someone who would ask me, "Does he bite?"

I would always assure them that he wouldn't. But one time a guy came walking by and asked the question. We had just left the church and I got to thinking about my answer. Finally, I said, "No . . . he doesn't bite; well at least not on Sundays." Haha! Of course, I never got to see his reaction but it was a fun moment for me.

Another time, I was traveling home from an engagement. We had a layover at the Dallas-Fort Worth Airport so we were deep underground near the terminals. We had been sitting around for a couple of hours when Birdie started "talking to me". He was trying to tell me he had to do his business. I ask you: where does one find grass in the middle of acres and acres of concrete?

So, my friend took the dog all the way out of the airport, through the front door, and halfway down the street. At last, they found a patch of grass for dear Birdie. When he was all done, he was more than ready to get back to Momma!

First, he had to go through the check-in area and the security check-point. And yes, they searched him for contraband—can you imagine? That was an exercise in patience for him. Then he had to wind through miles and miles of hallways, escalators and slow-moving people dragging their luggage behind them. But he flew through all the obstacles at top-notch speed!

You see when Birdie was separated from Momma for too long, he developed a good bit of anxiety. And when he wanted to get there, he wanted to get there *now*. He could actually bring my husband to his knees if he pulled hard enough, and David was over six feet tall. So, you can imagine my poor friend trying to hold him back! What a time that was!!

BIRDIE LOVED CHURCH

Birdie loved to go to church. In fact, everyone there used to call him "brother Birdie." If I was playing the piano some particular Sunday morning he would come and sit by me. Or if I was in the choir, he'd sit with me there. And of course, when I settled down in the pew, he was always right by my feet.

He really loved our Pastor too. I remember one time he just decided he would go see the Pastor while the choir was singing. He wandered over to the special chair on the platform where Pastor was seated and before we knew it, he jumped up on Pastor's lap. Well, he didn't exactly fit, but he snuggled up just as close as he could in front of God and everybody! It was his own special way of saying, "I love you." Everyone burst out laughing including the Pastor. It warmed all of our hearts.

Another thing Birdie loved were the eatin' meetin's. He was well behaved for the most part, but we're talking about food here. During mealtimes, he would sit patiently by my feet while everyone clicked their forks and stuffed their faces. Once in a while, I'd sneak him a scrap of something under the table and he was happy with that.

I'm sure he always had one eye on the buffet tables though. It didn't happen often, but we had caught him "counter-surfing" a couple of times. I guess he just wanted to see what was on the menu and maybe get a little sample. I did catch him trying it at home too. He definitely knew better, but he simply had to be reminded once in a while that this kind of behavior was not acceptable.

Another time, I remember we were in the car on our way to church. We were going to have a fellowship meal that day and so I had prepared a large casserole dish of macaroni and cheese. We secured it in the back of the SUV and there was still plenty of room for Birdie to climb in next to it. So, all was well as we made our way to the church. What we didn't know was at some point along the way, the lid to the casserole dish slipped off. When we got to church and went to pull the mac and cheese out of the back, we discovered that at least half of it was gone! My dear Birdie had helped himself to a very delightful entrée.

Overall Birdie was a smart, loving companion. In fact, I used to explain to folks that he was a "soul winner". How could that be, you ask? First of all, Birdie was a large, German Shepherd. He weighed over 75 pounds most of the time, and he had a big bushy coat that made him look even bigger.

Sometimes, I'd be walking along in Wal-Mart, shopping for this or that. Then I'd turn a corner to go down another aisle and inadvertently surprise someone who didn't expect to run into him. Romans 10:13 says, ***"For whosoever shall call upon the name of the Lord shall be saved,"*** (KJV). Well, that unassuming shopper would see the dog, pound their chest and cry out, "Lord, Jesus!" Poor folks. I know they were scared out of their wits, but I knew he was harmless and I'd chuckle under my breath.

GOD'S CONFIRMATION

I always knew I was meant to have Birdie. When I got him, they had already named him; he had to have a name for training purposes. So, when they brought him to me and told me his name was Birdie, I knew it was perfect. You see, my husband, David, played golf and "birdie" is a golf term. I felt it was God's confirmation that Birdie and I were meant to be together. Also, I used to raise cockatiels so my interest in birds was like another confirmation.

By the way, the term "birdie" means to get to the next hole in *one shot under par.* I guarantee you there was nothing *under par* about my Birdie. He was the most perfect guide dog a person could have, and he was perfect for me.

I was so blessed that Leader Dogs for the Blind in Rochester, Michigan gave me the opportunity to have Birdie as my guide dog. For those of you that might not know, this institution makes it possible for people who are blind and visually impaired to enhance their mobility, independence and quality of life.

The organization was founded by three Lions Club members. They have been providing guide dogs since 1939, and have proudly trained over 14,500 clients from 39 countries. Their mission is to empower people who are blind or visually impaired with lifelong skills for safe and independent daily travel. You can find them through the following website: http://www.afb.org/directory/profile/leader-dogs-for-the-blind/12

GOD'S TIMING

The day after my Birdie died, my son, David, was married. The wedding was October 27th, 2012. It's hard to understand God's timing sometimes, but I know His ways are higher than our ways. Maybe, while I had lost my friend, Birdie, I was gaining a new friend, Chelsey, (David's bride).

Speaking of timing and connections, God really does work out how people connect. My friend, Kathy, went to Toccoa Falls College. Her husband, Doug, was at the school back in 1977 when the water dam collapsed above the school, killing his daughter and 38 other people. One of the professors there at the time was a man named Norm Allison.

Just before David and Chelsey's wedding, Doug found out that Norm and his wife, Judy, are Chelsey's grandparents! It's so strange the way God has woven us together. He is so amazing!

CHAPTER TWENTY-EIGHT
BLESSED BEYOND MEASURE

SPECIAL PEOPLE

Along the way, God has put some very special people in my life and some very close friends. Kathy is one of those friends. She lets me talk to her about anything and she is never judgmental. She doesn't "freak out" over stuff. She's also trustworthy. She guards my privacy as much as I do and I appreciate that.

I've found Kathy to be true to her word, too. For example, she told me a long time ago, "If you ever need help, even in the middle of the night, you can always call me and I'll be there." Lots of people say it but not many mean it. They mean well but they can't be depended on when the rubber meets the road.

HELP IN THE NIGHT

One time, I found myself in trouble in the wee hours of the morning. I thought about who I could call and Kathy came to mind. She was in bed that night when the phone rang. She told her husband, "Mmm . . . it's Terri's number . . . look at the time. I know this is not going to be good."

She answered the phone and said, "Terri, what's the matter?"

I told her I had fainted and fallen in my bathroom. Then somehow, I managed to pull myself over to the bed in the other room to get my cell phone. And now I couldn't move.

Even in this moment God was taking care of me. If I had left the phone anywhere else I wouldn't have been able to call for help. It's amazing, but no matter how tough things get, He is there.

Without any more questions, she said, "Don't worry about a thing; I'll be right over." And she was.

It was well past midnight and she was 20 miles away but she and her husband came and managed to carefully lift me up off of the floor and put me on top of the bed. I was in a lot of pain. But at the same time, I hadn't lost my sense of humor. A certain TV commercial came to mind, and a phrase went through my head that said, "Help, I've fallen and I can't get up." I'm not sure why that was funny at the time, but it was.

They called an ambulance and followed it to the hospital where they discovered I had broken a hip. Kathy and her husband stayed with me until I was admitted. They probably got back home around five or six in the morning. It was a long night for them and not many would have stuck around like they did; they are true friends.

FAN OR FRIEND?

Kathy and I have a unique friendship. On the one hand, she's still a fan of Terri Gibbs. She remembers hearing Terri Gibbs on the radio when she was still living in Canada, years ago. But through our association at church, we have become close friends. She helps me with many things and I know I can count on her. That's hard to find in anyone.

It's great, too, that we seem to think alike. Often times she can anticipate what I need and she understands how I should be represented. We work well together because she separates all that fan stuff so that we can just be ourselves.

I've always had to discern whether someone was trying to be my friend or my fan. I've met people who have latched on to me for their own good, and then I'd wished I'd never trusted them. Because of being blind I've had to trust people a lot. But I've been blessed with good friends and I know God has looked out for me in this way.

CHAPTER TWENTY-NINE
MY LITTLE "B.J."

A PRECIOUS DAUGHTER

I had always hoped for a daughter. And BJ has always been a precious daughter to me. She has been a great help, often being "my eyes" when I have needed extra assistance. She has been a true blessing and a good friend.

BJ was like a second mom to my son, David, as well; there was fifteen years between them. She really was a big help when he came along.

In later years when I lost my husband, BJ was there for me. She was the best person in the world to talk to and I always found her so down to earth.

BJ once said how she felt about me. When I married her father, David, she said it was like getting a second mom. If she would have ever lost her real Momma, she knew she still had me to count on. It was special for her to have two mommas instead of just one.

We don't spend as much time together as we would like to because our lives are so busy, but I know that if I ever needed her, she'd be right there for me. I appreciate her so much.

DADDY'S GIRL

Hi, I'm B.J. I was fourteen when Terri and Daddy got married. I appreciated having Terri as a mom. I really admired her, too, and thought it was neat that she was so famous. I didn't have much musical ability myself. If I'd tried to make music, I would have sounded like an old tin can, even though my dad's brother, Dean Daughtry, is very talented. He's played

139

keyboard for the Atlanta Rhythm Section since 1971 and is one of the original founding members.

Whenever I was out with Momma, we'd often run into folks who realized she was the famous entertainer, Terri Gibbs. I would always try to protect her. She would usually be hanging on to my elbow so we could walk together. Then if somebody started staring, I'd give them one of those *looks;* you know what I mean? Then they'd quit.

For me, Terri is just *Momma* and I love her and would do anything for her. And I've always been so proud of the way she introduces me. She'll say, "This is my daughter, B.J."

MOMMA'S HELPER

Since I was already a teenager when Momma came into my life, we got to do fun things together like go shopping. I would help Momma pick out things for which she needed my eyes to see: like toothpaste and lady things. That was special for me. At home I enjoyed helping her with laundry, having the whites separated from the colored clothes, having permanent-press things separated, and having socks matched, and so on.

Sometimes Momma would ask me to take care of my little brother, David. I'd do things for him like bake his favorite cake with strawberry frosting on top. Momma did just fine when it came to baking, but she liked me to help her with the frosting. Using a rubber spatula, I would clean all the frosting from the inside of the bowl. Otherwise, Momma would have to scrape some out and then feel for more with her fingers and then scrape again. I always wanted to make things easier for her.

I remember when David was about two and a half or three. He was just big enough to reach up to the counter-top, and so he stood up on his tip-toes and pulled a whole cake down onto the floor, breaking the glass cake holder and lid. I cleaned up all the glass and everything off of the floor to make sure Momma didn't step in it. But then, as if nothing happened, David tugged at me and said, "Sissy, bake me another cake."

Having David as my little brother was a real trip! But I loved being his big sister. We did lots of fun things together even though he was fifteen years younger than me.

QUESTIONS

I used to wonder why Momma held her arms out in front of her when she walked around the house. I asked her once, "Momma, what's it like being blind?"

She told me, "BJ, just tape some cotton balls on your eyes and try to get around and see what you think about it." I did that for almost a day and it was quite an experience. I found myself holding out my arms like she did, trying to remember where the furniture was and how to find the hallway without bumping into everything.

I was also curious about another thing. I asked her, "Momma, what's your favorite color?" As soon as I said it, I thought to myself, "Oh, you idiot! Why did you ask her that?" That was so inconsiderate of me.

But she wasn't offended in the least. She thought about it for a minute and said, "I guess I'd have to say black."

"Why that color Momma?" I asked.

She said, "Well, I guess because that's the only color I've ever seen."

Growing up with Momma was wonderful. I loved her so much and I know she loved me.

HOME LIFE AND BEYOND

Just like David, I too loved coming home from school knowing Momma was always there. And I loved my daddy and was so proud that he was a school-bus driver. I always defended him if kids said anything bad about *the driver*. I'd let them know right away he was my dad and they'd better be careful what they said. It hurts me that Daddy is gone now but I'm so glad I still have Momma to turn to when I need someone.

I have to say, nothing compares to being raised by Momma and Daddy. They taught me so many things like the love of Jesus, how to love other people, and how to be good and kind. They gave me an understanding and a hunger for the things of God; I don't think I could have learned such things anywhere else.

I'll always remember one thing Momma said to me one day. She said, "BJ, I'm so glad to have you as my daughter." I knew she meant it from her heart and I cry just thinking about it. You see, she didn't treat me like her step-daughter but rather like her very own daughter. She made me feel secure and loved. And now that I'm married with stepchildren of my own, I'm glad Momma instilled those values in me; I can love them as my own without thinking otherwise.

Today, Momma's still the same. She takes my children, who aren't biologically hers, and holds them in her heart as her own grandchildren. She's Grandma, and don't let anyone forget it! She loves them; there's no doubt about it!!

Momma has molded me in ways that will be with me forever. So, I have to say, "Thanks, Momma, for

R. Douglas Veer/Terri Gibbs

being such a big part of my life. I don't know what I would have done without you as my example. I love you and will always know that I've been loved by you. I am truly blessed.

CHAPTER THIRTY
FROM A SON'S POINT OF VIEW – PART I

YOUNG DAVID AND HIS MOMMA

Hi, I'm David Wayne Daughtry the Second. Having a mother that's blind has changed my perspective on a lot of things. When I was a child in school, I was very social. And because I had a mother that couldn't see, I learned to be extremely descriptive and animated although a lot of times people thought I was just overly excited.

Also, I felt a bit strange sometimes compared to other kids. I'd say things like, "My mom and I went to such and such place on the weekend." I thought, "Wow, that's weird to be doing stuff with your mom like that." We'd go out to arcades or *put-put* together even though I thought you were supposed to do those things with your dad. Sometimes I'd spend time with other people and Mom would come along. I guess I developed a different perspective in that regard.

I used to help my mother quite a bit. I would often take her hand and put it on things for her to feel and recognize. I was doing that even before I could talk. I don't ever remember a time when I wasn't aware of her limitations. I always knew what needed to be done for her sake. If we were going somewhere and Daddy was busy doing something, I was always watching out for her, regardless of how excited or playful I was in the moment. It was just a natural thing for me.

One of my favorite things was coming home from school knowing my mom would always be there when I got off the bus. I'd run as hard as I could to get to the door and there she was. She always had a snack for me. Then we would do things together like watch T.V.

When I was really young, I used to like the program, *Barney the Purple Dinosaur.* We'd sit and watch it together and eat Graham crackers.

Now Daddy didn't get home until 4:30 or 5:00 o'clock, so before that, it was my time to hang out with Momma and I could get away with more stuff. It was like, "Yeah, you can go ahead and do that." But with Daddy, it was like, "Naw, you don't need to do that. Go clean your room or something." Yeah, I had to be a little more serious when Daddy came home.

PERFORMING CAME NATURALLY

We used to travel a fair bit. If my mom had to perform somewhere, the whole family went. And when she performed, it was strange to see how people reacted to her because it was normal for me. All I knew my entire life was us going and singing and being in front of people. So, when people would treat her all special, like "Gosh! That's Terri Gibbs!" I thought, "Hey, we're just doing what we do." I guess when I got to be in high school, things started changing because that's when she started slowing down. But prior to that, our traveling was a normal part of our lives.

She was good at what she did; she always loved Country music and did well at it. She came on the scene with Country roots but she had so much soul and blues that they didn't know where to put her.

It was so phenomenal that she could take a normal song and add some things to it and make it feel better. I think that's what posed a challenge for her producers and managers. She'd turn a song around and make it like "Wow," but how do you label that and sell that?

I'd find a song and say, "Momma check this song out." She'd listen to it and start playing it. Then a week

146

later she'd play it for me again and I would say, "Oh my God! You made that song 20 times better than what it was and I thought it was pretty good to start with."

And she plays these certain chords that go back to her playing by ear. She never really had extensive music lessons so she can't describe exactly what she's doing but she plays what fits the song. It's amazing that she hears all that. She's extremely smart.

I GOT THE MUSIC IN ME

I found myself being drawn to the guitar when I was 15 or 16 years old. It's kind of a funny story. Actually, when I was about 12 or 13, Momma and Daddy bought me a guitar for Christmas. I think they saw me playing around with one at my paw paw's (my dad's dad's) pawn shop. They'd have some musical instruments there from time to time and I'd pick up a guitar and pluck around on it, not knowing a single thing about it. So, I guess my folks saw me doing that, maybe more often than I thought.

One particular Christmas day, my folks gave me a guitar and I thought that was pretty cool. I took it to my room. Again, I didn't know anything about it. I pressed some strings and tried to strum it, but I lost interest really quickly. I played with it a couple of times and then just stuck it in the closet. I might have pulled it out, maybe once every four or five months. But it was like a toy that wasn't any fun because I didn't know how to work it.

Later when I was about 16, a new worship leader came to our church. He said, "Let's put together a praise team." He brought his guitar and it was the first time I had been around someone who could really play. I connected with that because I had seen guitar players before but they were performers on stage who were really good and not so approachable. The director's approach was such that he would say, "Let's start, and if you don't know how to make it work, I'll help you get started and show you some chords."

The funny thing was, I was becoming interested in the guitar again anyway. I remember getting it out of the closet one day. And when I grabbed the neck, my index finger went over the first string and my thumb went over the sixth string; both fingers were pressing down on the third fret. As I pulled it out of the closet, it swept across some clothes and it said, "brrrring". The guitar sounded out a "G" chord! (My fingers were actually in a "G" chord position except for one string.)

I was so surprised. I said, "Oh my gosh!" I just sat there, playing and playing and playing. Although I've become a lot more technical on the guitar, that's how I often play the "G" chord even to this day.

I know several guitar players but I just have to brag about one of them: Tanner Duckworth. Calling him a guitar player is an understatement. Oh, my goodness! He can even play two songs at once. It's crazy. He's an unbelievable talent. And he's only about 21 years old.

Someone said Tanner's up there with Chet Atkins, and I say easily; Tanner's that good. He blows me away. He's phenomenal. Just go to YouTube and type in Tanner Duckworth. You'll see and hear him play. I guarantee you will be amazed.

LAUNCHING OUT

From the time I started playing guitar at 16 until I graduated from high school, it was always in the back of my mind to try out the Country music thing just like

Momma. I knew it would be an option if I worked at it. And I did work at it, but I was never really committed to it. It was always more of a glorified hobby. One reason for that is my mom told me about some of her experiences in the music industry. She said the wisest thing I could ever do was to always have a backup plan. I thought about that a lot. I've always been a forward thinker and planner.

Prior to my senior year in high school, I was already planning ahead. I found myself on a straight track toward getting a construction and engineering degree. Those interests stemmed from when I was about thirteen and Mom would describe her big house on Chamblin Road. She still loves that house by the way.

We were sitting on her bed one day. The bed had a microfiber blanket. You could smooth it over in one direction but if you moved your fingers over it the other way, it made all the fibers stand up. I smoothed down the blanket and said, "Momma, draw out what you can, and show me the layout of that house."

Well, she obviously wasn't that great at drawing but she managed to show me where the different rooms were and how they were connected. I thought it was cool, so I grabbed some graph paper and completely drew out her house plan.

It really captivated me to the point that I wanted to explore other house plans. I started ordering magazines like *Two-Story Home Design*. And I'd go through them and pick out things I liked. I guess the interest was always there. Even as a young child I would have Lego's and stuff. I loved that kind of thing. It was fun to design and create things out of raw materials.

Leading up to my senior high school year I worked some construction jobs on the side and did some roofing. It seemed pretty lucrative at the time.

In my final year, I did a project for my Construction Management class. My teacher invited me to ride around with him to look at properties and check out contracting crews. He also described what the industry had been like in the past four or five years. So, I asked him, "How would I graduate high school, go to Georgia Southern for four years for construction management, graduate from there and start a construction company?"

He said, "David, I don't know if you realize this but the housing market is about to fall apart." I stopped in my tracks; I put on my brakes and said, "Whoa, what am I going to do!?" I found myself having to re-think my future.

CHAPTER THIRTY-ONE
FROM A SON'S POINT OF VIEW – PART II

COLLEGE BOUND

My Dad went into the hospital a few months before my high school graduation. I wasn't sure what his outcome would be; it turned out that he passed away in February and my senior project had to be completed by the end of the school year.

My heart was heavy with sadness. I was overwhelmed and quite discouraged. I thought, "I really don't know what to do now, but even if I did know what to do, what's the point?" That was my perspective on a lot of things. I thought, "You live life and you die. What's the point?" In the midst of all that I actually decided to enter college, but my attitude was poor and it got me off to a bad start.

It took a while, but I did begin thinking again about the benefits of college. I figured, when I finish, I'll get a little sheet of paper that'll mark the fact that I'll have just spent four years of my life to qualify me to do things other people may or may not be qualified to do. So, I felt I needed to get that college degree. I could still work on my music in the meantime. Then later, if I decided to take some kind of risk one way or the other, I would always have the other to fall back on.

GLAD FOR MY MUSIC ROOTS

Well, I'm glad I've had opportunities to play music along the way. I used to have a band that was based in Augusta, Georgia. We started playing at a neighbor's house; it was just some of us guys getting together. We weren't very serious about it. We were just hanging out. Then a friend of mine invited us to play at an upcoming duck-shoot, so we went and played a few songs.

We got together to play that one gig and didn't expect it to go anywhere. But we did so well that we said, "Hey, let's continue doing this." Then people started asking us to play here and there, like at Surry Center, a huge three-story shopping center in Augusta, or at birthday parties, or at the Columbia County Rodeo. We played a wedding just a year ago and it was good to get back together again. Since then, however, we've all gone in different directions.

COLLEGE LIFE

Today I still play, but it's usually just me and my guitar, playing acoustic stuff. I've played at the bistro in my town, and for the Department of Agriculture, as well as for some local establishments. I've played at Abraham Baldwin Agricultural College, (ABAC), where I attend, and some at the University of Georgia, (UGA).

Most of the time it's nothing I plan. Usually, someone will approach me and say, "Hey, would you mind doing this?" And I'll look at my schedule and see if I can. It's an opportunity to get away from all the pressures of school so I'll say yes. It lets me play a little music and relax for a while.

As for college, I have finally settled into a major and there's a story behind that. You see, I've always had a heart for farming. Grandma, my mom's momma, encouraged me in that direction at a young age. And that was even before I knew a lot about my great granddaddy having a dairy farm. Even on my dad's side, his father worked on a share-crop farm until World War II came around. Then he signed up for military service and that took him away from the farm.

I've said all that to say that I think it's in the blood; it really is. For whatever reason, the love of farming was passed down a couple of generations to me. I've always been enthralled by things of nature and things that grow. And I've always had a critical-thinking side to me as well.

My grandma started me at a young age, planting stuff around the house, preparing the soil, growing things, and learning how to fertilize them. At 12 or 13 years old, she was teaching me how to graft, or root, Boxwoods. She showed me how to feed the buds, put the plants in the sand, and keep them moist. There was always something different to do; it was really cool.

All of those experiences led me to ABAC College where I recently graduated with an undergraduate degree in Agriculture, and a concentration in Crop and Soil Science. Now I work in Advanced Technologies and Precision Agriculture.

I MARRIED MY SWEETHEART

I met my future wife, Chelsey, at school. She eventually graduated with a degree in Agriculture with a concentration in Livestock Production. Folks used to refer to us as the "dynamic duo" because of our degrees. I was proud to bring her home to meet Momma and they have developed a great relationship. Chelsey and I got married on Oct 27, 2012.

I also have to say that Chelsey has many qualities and has been successful with a lot of things. For example, one of her jobs was managing the calf farm at the UGA Research Center. I've been around cattle a lot and worked on a dairy farm for a while but Chelsey is gifted in the field. She has a way with animals far above the average person.

One day, she walked around a calf and said, "That calf's going to be sick in a couple of days."

I said, "That calf looks totally fine to me; I don't see a thing wrong with it."

She replied, "Well, if you look you can see how the ear is just a little bit bent and it's a little more moist on the nose than some of the other calves." I really didn't see it, but she sees minute details and pays attention to things. You know, she's the same way with people!

Now I'm not trying to compare my momma to a calf, but to put it into perspective, when Chelsey met Momma, she *read* her really fast and figured out what she needed. That helped them get off to a great start. Now she and Momma do girl things together and even get into trouble and all that good stuff! It really pleases me.

CHAPTER THIRTY-TWO
MORE THOUGHTS FROM DAVID AND CHELSEY

WHEN I MET TERRI

Hi, I'm Chelsey Daughtry. At first, I thought meeting Terri was a different sort of experience. Not necessarily because she was my mother-in-law, but in the sense of being able to relate. I had to "learn" her, and what she liked, and what she didn't like. I did figure out right away that she was very independent and didn't need a whole lot of help.

I'm so glad we have gotten to know each other; we actually got close quite quickly. And I've found we have a lot in common. We have a great relationship and we enjoy doing things together when we can.

REMEMBERING BIRDIE

It's with sadness that I remember Terri's dog, Birdie. It was the fall of 2012, and Birdie was nearing the end of his life. I was coming over to the house one day while Terri was gone to take care of Birdie. I had let him outside and after a time went to call him back in.

He was sitting at the bottom of the steps and acting kind of funny. I said, "Birdie, come on, come on," but he wouldn't get up. I went back in the house and told David something was wrong. We called Terri and let her know Birdie was not well. Of course, the story ended very sadly. As you know, Birdie was put to sleep a couple of days later and we were all so very heart broken.

This all happened in the month of October and David and I were in the middle of planning our wedding. It turns out that Birdie passed away on the day before we got married. David had to bring his body home and bury him and then we had to go to our wedding rehearsal. It was quite traumatic for me but just imagine how tough it was for Terri. Birdie was her best friend and he meant the world to her.

MISSING MOMMA

Now that I, (David) am not living at home, I miss being around my momma. I miss all the things that make her special. She does come to visit us pretty often even though we live about four hours away. But it's not the same.

The thing I miss most is that Momma always has some kind of idea about something every day. There's never a time when she quits thinking about something new and exciting. I swear, with all of her ideas--if she could see--she'd be an architect. She lives in her imagination so much. She's a dreamer and that's fun for me because I am too.

And I miss her spontaneity. For example, it might be evening time and Chelsey and I are outside doing something and Momma will come out and say, "What are y'all doing."

I'll say, "Not too much."

And she's like, "Do you want to go to the Huddle House?"

It'll be quite late and I'll say, "Momma, it's 11:00 o'clock!"

She's like, "Yeah, so come on, let's go!"

I also miss our sitting around and playing music together. That's a lot of fun. She likes my music for whatever reason and of course, I like her music for obvious reasons. Yeah, those things are enjoyable. I wish we could get together more often.

LOOKING TO THE FUTURE

I do worry about Momma even though she's got some phenomenal people who can help her in time of need. She actually does quite well on her own but it would be nice if we didn't live so far apart; it would be great if we could live closer to each other someday.

We've actually talked about sharing a home in the future and by then maybe Momma will be doing the "grand-baby" thing. I want to be able to buy enough property and build a nice mother-in-law suite right next to our house. There's always the option for us to all live together, but Momma's very independent so I know she would enjoy her own suite where she can have certain things a certain way, just the way she likes it.

A SPECIAL MOM

Momma and I are like best friends. If anything happens, I just call Momma and she prays about it. I've never lost anything she couldn't help me find. For example, one time while I was out hunting, I lost my wallet, so I asked Momma to pray about it. Six months went by and finally, a person found it and brought it to somebody else who knew me. He said, "What was the name?"

The finder said, "Uh, David Daughtry or something like that."

My friend said, "Really? Let me see that . . . oh my God! Yes, I know him." That was amazing!

If there's anything that stands out in my mind, it's my momma's perseverance. You can't tell her that she can't do something. Sometimes I'd put myself in her shoes and think, "Wow, that would be so difficult." But she has taught me to buckle down and get on with whatever I needed to do. She has always said,

"Perseverance will get you there. And if you can't do it easily, you can *still* find a way to get it done."

Yup, Momma is as tough as a yard hen. I remember one time, she started limping around the house and it kept up for a week or more. I said, "Momma, you're not getting any better!" So, she went to the doctor and he said, "You've got broken toes!!" What happened was Momma had tripped and thought it was just a sprain. She was in pain but she can handle an awful lot.

The flip side of the coin is that Momma can get a little hard-headed sometimes which causes me to seek her out for a sit-down talk. I'll say things like, "Momma, I know you've got M & Ms hiding in the drawer. Quit eating all that sugar." I still need to take care of her you know.

Another thing that's special is the way my momma meets people and develops relationships. She doesn't see what we see on the outside. I might question what a person is about and she'll say, "David, you need to get to know them; they're really a good person on the inside." She sees their true character in a way that I can't. She's helped me learn to look for that good things in people and that has inspired me in many ways.

I know folks love their moms but I feel as though I have been particularly blessed. I want to say, "Thank you, God, for letting me have such a wonderful Momma. And thank you, Momma, for being so special to me. I love you."

CHAPTER THIRTY-THREE
THE LOVE IS PASSED ON

FAMILY TIES

They say, "love is the tie that binds". And love has surely bonded our family together. As I look back through the pages of my life, I find that music has also linked us together. From the "all day Gospel singings" begun by my great grandfather to the precious moments spent with my son as we have shared songs with each other, I must say our family traditions haven't found a stopping place with me. My son continues to carry on the legacy.

Yes, my son, David has grown a lot since he was that little guy spreading salt and pepper all over the house. He's grown and grown and grown into a six-foot-five young man, and a fine young man he is. He has found his way in life. That is, he's committed to investing in his education and he knows it will serve him all of his days. And he continues to bless people with his music. I'm so proud to be his mom.

Other traditions and interests have also been passed down. Just like Granddaddy with his dairy farm, David is interested in farming, and so is his wife, Chelsey. I'm so encouraged for them both. David and Chelsey have a great future ahead and I can't wait to see how the Lord is going to order their steps.

MY LATEST PROJECT

As for me, I continue to make music and try to use the gift God has given me. My latest album, *Sum It All Up*, was released in June 2017. I actually started working on it in 2013. I prayed a very long time about this album because I really needed God's direction. It had been awhile since I had done any recording and I really wanted Him to be in it. Not that I didn't want the Lord to be in all of my records. It's just that I wanted this album to make a statement: that is when I "sum it all up", nothing is more important than having Jesus at the center of my life.

NO LONGER IN THE DARK

I once lived my Christian life in the dark because I was overly attached to worldly things but I didn't know it at the time. Looking back, I used to wonder what I had gained from doing shows, as enjoyable as they were. But the applause and the accolades didn't touch the emptiness I often felt.

Some entertainers make money and fame their god, but if that's all there is then their fulfillment lasts only until their last movie is forgotten or their last hit song is gone.

I had it all too, but none of it will matter when I get to Heaven. All that will really matter is my knowing Jesus, and knowing He loves me no matter what. That's what I want people to know. "He's my comfort, my refuge, my fortress, and the love of my life. Nothing in this world can take me away from that relationship with Him."

There are so many distractions and temptations that can draw us away from the Lord. But there's nothing better than having God as the director of your life. He will never lead you the wrong way and He will always show you where you need to be. He helps hold back temptations so they can't destroy you. But you must be completely surrendered to Him. You can't go on living in your own strength.

The Holy Spirit of God has filled my heart in a very real way, causing me to want to please Him more than anything. That has meant *giving* Him everything including my music. I want my music to count for Him.

Yes, the light of Jesus has enlightened me exposing the darkness of my sins. The Bible says, **"I was blind, but now I see,"** (John 9:25; NIV). Even though I'm blind, I no longer walk in darkness, spiritually speaking.

WHEN I GET TO HEAVEN

One day I'm going to knock on Heaven's door and God will say, "Welcome home Terri, my faithful daughter. I have a place prepared for you". Then I'll see my friends, my family, and my loved ones. I'll see all the people in my life that have accepted Christ's love just like I have. And we shall dwell in the presence of the Lord forever.

Last but not least, I look forward to that awesome day when blindness will be no more. A marvelous new life will be waiting for me in Heaven. It'll be better than a dream; I can hardly wait!

I've had people ask me what I see when I dream, and what I picture in my mind when I talk about things here on earth. The truth is, all I can see is what I can touch and then make the best of that in my imagination. One day that will change. Just think of it: I'll get to see the black and white of the piano keys and the colors of the rainbow. I'll be able to see the faces of my loved ones . . . it's something I'm looking forward to.

The first thing I'll see of course will be Jesus. I'll look at Him with a clear vision and what a sight He will be! I've been in darkness all of my life but when I get to heaven, I'll never be in darkness again. There will be no more night, no more darkness, and no more tears. The day will be eternal. How amazing is that?

I've never seen the sunlight, but then I'll see the Light of the Son. His presence alone will light the heavens. We'll walk with Him, and talk with Him, and sing songs of praise to His name.

SOMEBODY'S KNOCKIN'

Revelation 3:20 (TLB) says, ***"Look! I stand at the door and knock. If you hear my voice and open the door, I will come in, and we will share a meal together as friends."***

(Verse 21; CEV), ***"Everyone who wins the victory will sit with me on my throne, just as I won the victory and sat with my Father on his throne."***

****

If you haven't experienced Jesus in your life, I wish you would. He took all of your sin and mine upon Himself so that we could be forgiven and live in fellowship with Him.

If you'll ask, He will come into your heart, forgive you, and give you the most amazing peace you could ever have. And when this life is over, He promises you eternal life with Him.

Listen very carefully now, as He stands and knocks at the door of your heart. Will you answer Him? Will you accept His love? Will you give Him your heart? Why not say "Yes"? Your whole life will change for the better and you'll wonder why you waited so long.

SINNER'S PRAYER

"Dear God, I know that I have sinned
and am deserving of punishment.
But because You loved me so much,
You sent Your only Son,
Jesus Christ, to die on the cross for me.
Thank you that you raised Him to life
on the third day and that He now
reigns in Heaven forever more.
With your help, I place my faith and trust
in Jesus as my Savior and Lord.
Please forgive me
and come into my heart.
With your help, I will live for you
from this day forward.
In Jesus' name I pray, Amen!"

BLESSINGS TO YOU!

If you just prayed this prayer, I'd like to be the first to welcome you into the family of God. And I'd like to ask you to do one more thing. Would you go tell someone that you've just become a Christian? Tell them how it happened; share your experience with someone. It's so important to confess your encounter with Jesus to others. In fact, if you have just made this decision for Christ, I would love to hear from you. You can contact me at terri@terriGibbs.us.

I may not ever meet you but please know I love you in Jesus just as Jesus loves me. I look forward to one day seeing you in Heaven. Then I'll look you in the eye and tell you how glad I am to be your sister in Christ. May God richly bless you!

BIOGRAPHY OF TERRI GIBBS

As a singer, musician, and songwriter, Terri Gibbs has enjoyed the success of Nashville and the entertainment world. Between 1980 and 1990, she recorded seven studio albums, including four projects for MCA Records and one for Warner Brothers. During that time, she also charted 13 singles on the Billboard Country singles charts, including her original debut single, *Somebody's Knockin'*, which reached number eight on the country charts, number thirteen on the pop charts and number three on the Adult Contemporary charts.

In addition to the Country Music Association Award, Terri's numerous awards include the Academy of Country Music's first-ever Horizon Award given in 1981 which recognizes the best new artist of that year. Accolades poured in including a nomination for a Grammy.

Miss Gibbs also entered the Country Top 20 charts with *Rich Man, Mis'ry River, Ashes to Ashes,* and *Anybody Else's Heart but Mine.*

Later on, Terri returned to her Gospel roots. In 1987 she recorded the Grammy-nominated album *Turn Around*. The single by the same name was successful on the Contemporary Christian Music charts, as was the single, *I Can See Heaven*. After the Warner Brother's album, *Old Friends,* Terri left Country music for good, signed a contract with Word Music, a Christian company, and has never looked back.

In November of 2012, Terri performed during the Artists Music Guild's Heritage Awards and at the end of her performance, was presented with a Lifetime

Achievement Award for her years of dedication. She had no prior knowledge of winning and it truly blessed her heart.

Terri Gibbs continues to record Gospel albums and perform where ever the Lord leads her, pouring her heart out through the beautiful voice God has blessed her with. She does it all for Jesus, the Lord of her life. She also looks forward to sharing her music with you!

Below is her discography and list of singles released.

DISCOGRAPHY

Albums
1981 Somebody's Knockin'
1981 I'm A Lady
1982 Some Days It Rains All Night Long
1983 Over Easy
1985 Old Friends
1985 The Best of Terri Gibbs
1987 Turn Around
1988 Comfort the People
1990 What a Great Day
2002 No Doubt About It
2010 Your Grace Still Amazes Me
2014 The Best of Terri Gibbs (re-released)
2017 Sum It All Up

Singles
1980 Somebody's Knockin'
1981 Rich Man
1981 I Wanna Be Around
1981 Mis'ry River
1982 Ashes to Ashes
1982 Some Days It Rains All Night Long
1982 Baby I'm Gone
1983 Anybody Else's Heart but Mine
1983 Tell Mama
1985 A Few Good Men
1985 Someone Must Be Missing You Tonight
1985 Rockin' In A Brand Cradle

1987 Turn Around
1987 I Can See Heaven
1988 Comfort the People
1988 Unconditional Love
1988 Promised Land
1991 One to Grow On
2017 Brother Joe

Purchase music by Terri Gibbs at:
https://store.cdbaby.com/Artist/TerriGibbs

EPILOGUE

Terri Gibbs is a precious living soul who loves music, loves the sound of the piano, and especially loves singing praises to Jesus. Many have sat and cried at the beautiful, godly sentiment in Terri's voice. Folks could listen to her sing all day long.

One of Terri's most special performances was at the 1994 Bill Gaither Home-Coming. It blessed everyone when she sang *The First Thing I'll See,* (Available on Video: *Sunday Go to Meeting Time-1996*). She has also performed this song at many of her concerts. It would be only fitting to let others who have met her, share their comments here. So here they are, unchanged and printed as they originally appeared.

Don Weathersbee
The First Thing I'll See is my favorite song of hers, especially watching all the old timers from the Gaither homecoming group, tearing up. When you watch them one by one, many of the old timers have "gone home". These videos make you miss them even more than the old-style photos. The videos help us enjoy and remember them, even though they're gone. Thanks for your love for Terri.

Joe Acord
My favorite Gospel song of all-time. It's a perfect song. She has been blind from birth and wrote this song herself when she got saved and became a born-again Christian. She is so talented as a singer, writer, and piano player. I can listen to it over and over again.

Chandra Hollison
This song has touched my soul. What a beautiful lady.

Eddie
I've seen this video many times; it brings tears to my eyes every time.

Joe Todd
She sang this, at our church last weekend. What a great song for her to sing. Thanks, Terri. You go gal.

Mrmusicfromthestars
This is so wonderful, especially because, as noted below, she has been blind all her life. One of her best recordings in my opinion. There's no doubt she means every word and I listen to it often as well. Inspiring. A wonderful singer who deserves to be much more successful.

Donna Reid
I Love her to death. I think she's wonderful. :-)
Love u, Terri.

Marshamc
So very moving. Terri Gibbs always sings straight from
the heart. Thanks so much.

Vernon
Somebody knocked! It was Jesus, and she let him
come into her heart to live forever! What a great song.
It brings me to joyful tears! So powerful by a very
gifted singer thanks for sharing.

FINAL THOUGHTS

THE AUTHOR

So, here is the very heart of Terri Gibbs as I know her. Her faith in God inspires all who have ever heard her deep, velvet voice. You don't have to listen very long to know that what you're hearing is the love of Jesus coming through her words as she sings to glorify Him.

The world may think of Terri as being blind but her spiritual vision is as clear as a bell. Her music reaches the spiritually blind. It points the way to Christ as the only true One who offers love, mercy, and forgiveness. Even the most hardened souls can find that pathway to salvation through Jesus.

Terri walks the path of her faith by the light of her trusted Savior. All who have ever been blessed by Terri's singing will have seen Gods' light shining through her very being.

And Terri, here's a personal note to you: Please know that we love you with genuine Christian hearts and we will continue to pray that God will bring you a multitude of blessings and always hold you close to Himself. May you continue to serve Him with the beautiful gift He has given you.

–R. Douglas Veer; blessed friend and Christian brother

A NOTE FROM TERRI

Well . . . this is who I am and this is where my roots are planted. You've met my momma and daddy, my brothers, my husband, my son, my daughter, my daughter-in-law, and some of my closest friends.

Please let me say thanks to all of you, my wonderful family, friends, and fans who have been such great supporters. I've had so many amazing people in my life. I truly appreciate each of you.

If God would grant my greatest wish, it would be to see--not necessarily with earthly eyes but with heavenly eyes--to see you in Heaven one day. The song says, "The first thing I see will be Jesus," but then I look forward to meeting up with each of you once again as well.

Thank you all and may God bless you richly and warmly with His wonderful love.

--Terri

PHOTOS

Terri as a baby - November 1955

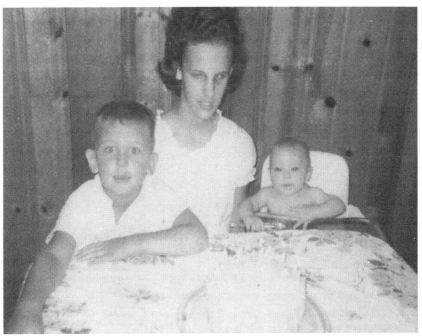

Terri--aged 13--with her two brothers

Terri performing at her high school (Butler High)

Terri Gibbs' high school

Terri performing at the Bell Auditorium
in Augusta, GA

Terri with Dolly Parton

Terri Gibbs - promo photo

Terri - singing at Border's Bookstore

Terri's family: husband David (left),
Son David (right), guide dog "Birdie"

Terri and "Birdie

MUSIC

Purchase music by Terri Gibbs at:
https://store.cdbaby.com/Artist/TerriGibbs

BOOKING
If your church or organization would like to book TERRI GIBBS for a concert, you can reach her at the following email address:
terri@terrigibbs.us

YOUR OPINION COUNTS!

If you have enjoyed this book,
please consider
**writing a short book review
at Amazon.com**
Help us spread the word,
and share Jesus with others too!

Made in the USA
Columbia, SC
21 January 2020